D1271165

HOW PSYCHO-THERAPY HEALS

COMMENTARY

This is my easiest, clearest, and most immediately accessible book in the field of psychotherapy. I am delighted to see it reprinted, as I think it fills a need for the novice as an introduction to the discipline of intensive psychotherapy. The section on existential anxiety is especially important for the student who comes to the subject from non-medical disciplines such as psychology, social work, or theology. I hope the student will go on to a further study of the subject in my books *The Technique and Practice of Intensive Psychotherapy* and *Freud Teaches Psychotherapy*; however, this volume is indeed the place to start. It presents a painless and nontechnical introduction to the subject, suitable for anyone with a college education.

Richard Chessick, M.D., Ph.D.

HOW PSYCHO-THERAPY HEALS

The Process of Intensive Psychotherapy

by Richard D. Chessick, M.D.

Jason Aronson Inc.
Northvale, New Jersey
London

To George Gomori

Tu se' lo mio maestro e 'l mio autore;
tu se' solo colui da cu' io tolsi
lo bello stilo che m' ha fatto onore.

Inferno (Canto I)

New Printing 1987

ISBN: 0-87668-821-0

Library of Congress Catalog Number: 77-91953

Manufactured in the United States of America.

ACKNOWLEDGMENT

The author would like to express appreciation to the following for their many helpful suggestions toward the preparation or publication of the book: Jason Aronson, M.D.; Carl Christensen, M.D.; Stanford Gamm, M.D.; Peter Giovacchini, M.D.; Robert Marsh; and Daniel Schiff, M.D.

The residents in psychiatry over the past 10 years at Northwestern University and at the Illinois State Psychiatric Institute have been instrumental in the production of this work through their many vital, original, and penetrating questions in our seminars on psychotherapy, and by their patient listening to and detailed criticism of the lectures on which the present manuscript is based. Similar acknowledgment is due to the medical students at Northwestern University and both nursing students and graduate nurses at the Veterans' Administration Research Hospital and Passavant Hospital in Chicago, Illinois, and The Forest Hospital, Des Plaines, Illinois.

The author and publisher wish to thank the following journals for permission to include materials published by them: *Psy-*

chiatry Digest, The American Journal of Psychotherapy, and *Voices.*
This material consisted of paragraphs, with corrections, drawn
from Chessick, 1965, 1967a, 1967c, which appear in Chapter 10,
and from Chessick, 1965, 1966, 1968, which appear in Chapter 12.
(See the Bibliography for complete citation of source.)

CONTENTS

Canst thou not minister to a mind diseas'd,
Pluck from the memory a rooted sorrow,
Raze out the written troubles of the brain,
And with some sweet oblivious antidote
Cleanse the stuff'd bosom of that perilous stuff
Which weighs upon the heart?

Macbeth (Act V, Scene III)

PART I

Basic Considerations

1

Introduction

How does psychotherapy heal? More specifically, what is it in the process of intensive psychotherapy that leads to the basic mental reorganization we call "cure"—a genuine improvement in the patient's adaptative capacities and the realization of his potential for love, productivity, and recreation.

This book hopes to contribute toward raising the standards of teaching psychotherapy to psychiatrists, medical students, psychologists, nurses, social workers, and clergy by presenting a detailed discussion of aspects of psychotherapy that are usually glossed over in ordinary training and in standard texts. It will focus mainly on the relatively obscure and undiscussed aspects of intensive psychotherapy, with only a brief review of what has already been covered in standard texts. It is hoped that the reader will emerge from this work with a better knowledge of the set of crucial factors vital to the catalysis of psychic healing in the process of psychotherapy and with a more definite idea of what he is and is not trained and equipped to do.

Certain basic assumptions are at the foundation of this work. The fundamental concepts of psychoanalysis regarding the structure and functioning of the personality are taken as the most useful set of definitions and heuristic concepts to enable us to communicate our experiences with patients. Detailed review of such concepts is unnecessary here and may be found in any basic textbook of psychoanalysis such as Brenner (1955) or Fenichel (1945).

It would have been the simplest procedure merely to review some of the flurry of recent publications on the subject of individual psychotherapy, in order to present the consensus on the crucial factors. In fact, an excellent review of the pertinent current literature has already appeared, by Wallerstein (1966). However, as clinical experience accumulates and reading knowledge deepens and broadens over the years, the regretful conclusion forces itself upon the thoughtful therapist: there simply is no consensus on certain vital issues. One cannot develop a synthesis of various methods without doing violence to some important views.

This makes it necessary to appeal directly at times to the therapist's own clinical experience. Otherwise, as Orr (1954) points out in his attempt to review the definition of countertransference, there could be ". . . little more than a catalogue of points of view." It will be specified throughout the text when personal experience is being directly utilized in the discussion.

There are enormous gaps in our knowledge and obvious dangers in appealing to "clinical experience," but in the absence of consensus or experimental proofs it is the best one can do. Thinking carefully through what one is trying to do is infinitely better than doing psychotherapy with no conscious *clear* idea of what one is trying to do or how one is trying to do it. Just stumbling along in psychotherapy happens more often than is admitted. The same stumbling can occur when the therapist insists on holding blindly and rigidly to any dogmatic theory that he has not examined freshly for himself and kept under continuous review in the light of new clinical experience.

The lack of curiosity about the details of just how psychotherapy heals, in so many people who are practicing psychotherapy, is most impressive and rather alarming. Many practitioners of this discipline, partly a science and partly an art, seem content to drift along with clichés and half-truths learned in training, without modifying or deepening their understanding by clinical experience. What a contrast to Freud—the founder of modern psychotherapy—who was constantly questioning, revising, and learning from his experience and who did not hesitate to discard even his own previous convictions when the clinical material as he saw it forced him to do so.

The ultimate loser in this situation is the patient. Freud (1912) attempted to demonstrate his attitude by describing his method primarily as *research*—do your research into understanding the patient as carefully as you can and the "therapy" will take care of itself. Of course, as is evident from his own behavior described in his famous case histories, he didn't mean this to be as cold as it sounds, but the basic spirit it expresses is quite valid. We all know that direct efforts to "mother" or give "tender loving care" to a patient fail for the most part—even Sechahaye's (1951) method is called *symbolic* realization—and that if there is to be permanent change a more indirect and complex process must take place. It is obvious that at least the intellectual structure of this process must be an attempt to understand—but how complex this simple phrase can really be, and how completely the patients can distort our attempts to understand in order to suit purposes of their own!

The basic reason for the prevalence of traditionalism, dogma, and bureaucratic routine in the practice of psychotherapy is poor and inconsistent training in psychotherapy that goes on in many training programs in psychiatry, psychology, social work, and pastoral counseling. There is an enormous variety of training for psychotherapy, ranging, as Guiora *et al.* (1967) point out, ". . . from the long and arduous road of psychoanalytic training to the scanty exposure and minimal education of the self-appointed enthusiast." Psychotherapy is not yet taught as a body of knowledge or a consistent discipline in many medical centers or graduate training schools, the way one might expect it to be. Compare, for example, the teaching of pharmacology across the country; yet just as consistent a body of knowledge could be gathered and utilized as the basis of teaching psychotherapy.

In addition, there is no set of minimal standards for the psychotherapist and no qualifying examination of any kind. The public has no way of knowing whether a given psychotherapist has even a smattering of understanding of what he is doing. Various training programs emphasize psychotherapy of different kinds in many scattered ways, ranging from numerous carefully planned courses and intensive supervision to giving the new resident a set of keys for the locked ward—often with 80 to 120 patients jammed in it—and telling him to go ahead and learn.

Although most of the criticism from the medical profession directed to psychiatrists today is heaped upon the dogmatic theorists, these actually represent only a dwindling minority of psychiatrists. The greatest danger to the public comes from psychiatrists and other professionals trying to do "long-term psychotherapy" without having had rigorous training in psychotherapy. For example, it does not follow that, because one has spent three years in a residency seeing many and varied cases of psychopathology that one knows how to do psychotherapy. The absolute minimum of qualifications, which are not provided in many residencies in psychiatry and not required on psychiatry board examinations in an explicit fashion, are to have experienced a personal psychotherapy and to have undergone substantial supervision of intensive long-term psychotherapy. (The optimum ratio of such supervision is 1 hour of supervision to 3 hours of therapy with patients.) It is not enough to see "follow-up" patients (who have been released from the hospital) for a few months just to adjust their drug dosages and the like.

Intensive individual long-term psychotherapy is a specific discipline that must be learned through supervised experience after one is healthy enough to at least hear what the patient is saying part of the time. It is possible to go through a psychiatric residency successfully today without any significant experience in this discipline and without attaining the prerequisite level of health.

Unfortunately the public can only judge by position, rank, affluence, and reputation. Take, for example, the case of a young woman who needed to be protected against her deep wish to regress by the bolstering of her superego. Her ego was so weak for many years that she managed to function only through the sense of duty and the fear—that she generated in herself—of authority figures. She got married and the new responsibilities led to an overwhelming inundation by her regressive wishes with enormous guilt and consequent depression. She went to a well-known psychiatrist, a person of influence and importance in the medical community. The psychiatrist reacted in a stereotyped manner to the depression in this borderline patient, and recommended immediate hospitalization. The patient at once became much worse as the regressive temptations were increased by the idea of hospitalization. Somehow there was some ego left and she refused hospitalization and went instead to another psychiatrist, equally well-known and with a similar excellent reputation. This one heard her, was stern although kindly, and in two sessions in his office the "depression" was gone temporarily.

This is *not* a case that can be explained as due to the patient's and the psychiatrist's undergoing various transference and countertransference reactions. In this situation the first psychiatrist had no training in psychotherapy but a lot of training and experience in psychiatric administration, diagnosis, and somatic treatment. Her approach was the "kindly old general practitioner" approach. In other words she did what any decent general physician might do in the situation. She made a diagnosis and prescribed hospitalization on the basis of the diagnostic picture, without regard to the dynamic details of the case. This technique works in a large percentage of cases, making it possible to practice psychiatry without training in long-term psychotherapy. In the borderline case, however, as has been described by the author (1965, 1966, 1968), such static techniques most often lead to failure in the treatment.

If one is a "kindly old general practitioner" and one has gone through a residency and learned diagnosis and somatic and short-term follow-up treatment, as well as how to allow acutely psychotic patients to pull themselves together in the hospital, one can successfully practice psychiatry. However, one will get into trouble with treatment of the increasingly large group of borderline cases or whenever one attempts intensive long-term psychotherapy.

In summary, this book assumes that a body of generally accepted knowledge on the subject of intensive long-term psychotherapy now exists and can be clearly communicated to professional students who will be engaged in psychotherapy of one form or another. In addition, the author's clinical experience will be called on to delineate controversial areas in intensive long-term psychotherapy and outline alternatives and possible solutions.

Therefore the professional reader, regardless of background in social work, psychology, or medicine, will hopefully understand better what intensive long-term psychotherapy is and how it heals. This can be useful both to those who wish to practice this discipline and to those who wish to clearly restrict their psychotherapeutic work to shorter or less intensive procedures.

The greatest danger is to "drift" into intensive long-term involvements with patients without a clear idea of what one is trying to do. This is both unprofessional and dangerous, since it can lead to expensive stalemates that harm both the patient and therapist when they are finally broken up. Often these stalemates are self-perpetuating, for the hostile dependency upon which they are based leads to a threat of serious acting out or even acute psychosis when the possibility of separation arises. The "sadomasochistic analytic couple" (Greenson and Wexler 1969) is an example of such a stalemate.

It is obvious, therefore, that therapists who wish to embark upon an intensive long-term relationship with patients are assuming a great responsibility and should understand what they are doing as much as possible.

2

Emotional Maturity

Before turning to a close examination of "intensive long-term psychotherapy," it is logical to begin with a brief examination of the concepts of "mental health," "emotional maturity," and "mental illness."

In this work the term "mental health" is used synonymously with the term "emotional maturity," implying a focus on the development or maturation of certain aspects of the personality. If this development unfolds properly and reaches a mature state, the individual automatically has what is called "mental health." Psychotherapy deals with miscarriages of this development, both in terms of the consequences of such miscarriages and the factors causing the miscarriage.

To illustrate the concept of mental health or emotional maturity further, it is useful to review the well-known clinical questions that are employed to assess mental health in a superficial manner. In the case of a child, for example, we try to answer some typical questions:

(1) At what stage of development is the child and what are the developmental levels of the conflicts the child is showing? Obviously, these should correspond.

(2) How much surplus energy does the child have for growth and play?

(3) How much flexibility and how much capacity does the child have to shift and change routines?

(4) How does the child deal with frustration?

In adults one may ask a set of similar but more detailed and complex questions. If the adult is showing conflicts, at what developmental level are they? Do his symptoms represent a fixation at a certain developmental level or a regression from a more basic conflict at a higher developmental level? How much can the adult distinguish between fantasy and reality?

How does the person relate to other people and perceive others and himself (ego-object relationships)? Can he differentiate an individual here now from someone out of the past to a reasonable extent?

How does the ego deal with social values and controls? How does the ego deal with the superego? One must also investigate whether the person is able to differentiate the past values of childhood from his present values as an adult.

How does the ego deal with the impulse life? What are the energies and strengths of the various impulses and how are they handled? So, for example, can the individual postpone gratification? Can he stand need-tension and regulate the discharge of needs? Also, how primitive and disorganized are the person's impulses?

A detailed discussion of the stages of development and the pathological problems that can arise at each stage is beyond the scope of this work. The reader is referred to English and Finch (1957), to English and Pearson (1963), and Lidz (1968) for such information.

For a much deeper look at the subject, Saul (1960) has devoted an entire volume to the concept of "emotional maturity." In a more recent paper (1966) he describes his conception of the *development* of emotional maturity, which is vital to any discussion of how psychotherapy heals. He writes:

Development to maturity proceeds of its own nature. . . . The fundamental condition for human emotional maturation, assuming adequate food and physical care, consists of: (a) good feelings towards the child and (b) good examples of mature behavior on the part of those responsible for the child and closest to it. . . . The child's pattern of feelings towards its parents and siblings, which is formed by about age six, *remains constant for life* in its essentials. This pattern sets channels for the child's developing feelings towards others and toward itself. *And it continues as a permanent nucleus, mostly unconscious, in the personality. The child we once were lives on in each of us however much of the rest of the personality matures.* (Italics added.)

These "basic hypotheses" of Saul have to be qualified by reference to the as yet unknown constitutional elements that enable some people to be warped more easily than others. The capacity for responsivity to human stimuli and the biological quantity of basic energy directed toward growth and survival seem to be vital, genetically determined aspects of the personality.

It is now common knowledge that mental illnesses are not the result of a single traumatic experience although there are such entities as "traumatic neuroses" seemingly precipitated by a single event in a person predisposed by earlier factors. Most mental illness is occasioned by the summation of numerous small incidents and from the total "atmosphere" within which the individual's ego develops and solidifies to form his adaptive mechanisms of behavior.

A seriously upsetting experience that happens in a home in which there is an atmosphere of good mothering has a far less significant effect than a relatively minor event that happens in an atmosphere of bad mothering. People tend to hang their difficulties on one or two events, but that is only the nature of human thinking, which only too often commits the "fallacy of misplaced concreteness" (Whitehead 1941). It is much more difficult to conceive of and to describe a whole atmosphere.

Both "good mothering" and "good fathering" are very important in the creation of a desirable atmosphere in which the child's ego can develop. The basic aspects of good mothering and good fathering are well known and reviewed in the texts on development mentioned above, but recently there has been an increasing concentration on ego development in the first few years of life. Certain aspects of the mother-child interaction seem to have a profound effect on the basic core of the personality.

Since the mother is the early source of reassurance and of security from anxiety (later this source may be generalized to the well-known transitional objects), a flood of anxiety from *any* cause during the early period of life could therefore fixate the infant on the need to remain close to mother. This anxiety* could come from genetic problems involving excessive need or from actually inadequate maternal love as described above.

The infant does not at first recognize the mother as a discreet person, but only as a source of relief from anxiety, so it is not a paradox that he would cling more tightly to her as a consequence of inadequate maternal love. Anxiety, therefore, becomes the primary motivating force behind clinging to the symbol or fantasy "mother"; once this bond is fixated the patient will die rather than give it up, for, as Knapp *et al.* (1966) point out, death is conceived of as a reunion with the beautiful (all-loving) mother.

These conceptions are supported and placed in the fifth or sixth month of life in a careful review by Brody and Axelrad (1966). At this point the mother is clearly recognized as an object of relief from anxiety and the infant also becomes aware of the possibility of her absence. This actually develops first in a prior phase in the first six weeks of life, during which occurs the imprinting of the mother as a species-specific object, but it is in a second imprinting phase at about five or six months that she becomes imprinted as an individual, connected specifically with relief of anxiety. As the authors point out in a passage again reminiscent of Saul:

* "Anxiety," as used in this text, is understood on the basis of the "signal theory" of Freud (1926). For a summary of recent conceptions and experiments on "anxiety" see Chessick *et al.* (1966a, 1966b), and Chessick (1967b). See also Chapter 11.

Should this set of statements be verified, it is implied that early infantile experiences are of far-reaching and permanent significance for the structuring of the affective as well as the intellectual destiny of the individual.

If Saul's conception of emotional maturity is correct, as we have every clinical reason to believe, then the interaction between genetic endowment, instinctual drives, and early infantile experiences is the crucial one toward the determination of future mental health.

Intensive long-term psychotherapy must deal with the basic pattern of attitudes and feelings developed first in the mother-infant symbiosis and then fixed into a "core" or nuclear personality through further childhood experiences with both parents and siblings. Psychotherapy is directed toward the permanent "nucleus," or "the child that lives on in each of us."

Saul writes (1966):

> If this psychodynamic nucleus or core of feelings is basically loving and if the relations with parents and siblings remain loving, then the child matures smoothly and adequately. The child becomes a loving spouse, parent, friend, and citizen—a responsible productive man or woman of good will. The helpless, dependent child has developed into the inwardly secure, responsible, giving parent. The seedling matured into a straight full tree.

A great many influences later in life can determine the final set of feelings with which an individual is endowed. A healthy father or a change of mother, for example, can ameliorate an impaired early childhood. A fortunate identification with an uncle or a teacher in adolescence, marriage to a healthy loving person, or even a lucky circumstance such as an empathic or understanding employer can do much to cover over or even neutralize a pathological childhood nucleus.

The stress is placed here on the childhood nucleus, for if intensive long-term psychotherapy is to be truly curative rather than ameliorative, it must affect this core. Otherwise in times of stress the pathology will manifest itself again.

When we speak of curative processes in psychotherapy, we do not address ourselves to any "diseases," since in psychiatry there are no specific "diseases" but only preponderant pathological reaction patterns, appearing as personality characteristics or clusters of symptoms, or both. These in turn are manifestations of emotional immaturity, or, to put it more formally, they reflect an impaired formation of the ego.

Mental illness is based on the unhealthy development of ego functions. For example, the autonomy of the nondefensive functions of the ego is constantly interfered with by the energic demands of the defensive structures (Roazen 1968). The capacity of the ego to endure frustration, delay, ambiguity, separation, and misery is significantly reduced and the "plasticity" of the ego is impaired. There is a disorder among the functioning parts of the personality and consequently a failure of relationships between the individual and other people.

The roots of all severely unhealthy ego functions are found in the mother-child symbiosis in the first year of life. However, subsequent relationships both with parents and with siblings can also substantially affect ego development before a "hardening" of the core or nucleus of the personality takes place, by about the sixth year of life.

Further experiences in later life with significant people can ameliorate or cover over those warps in the ego functions developed early in life, but only the most unusual experiences can reach back through the years and substantially change the childhood nucleus within the personality. The most important of these experiences is the intense interaction of long-term psychotherapy, and we say that this process has "cured" or "healed" a patient only when a fundamental change in the childhood core of the personality has been brought about, as reflected by substantial improvement in ego function.

3

Psychoanalytically Oriented Psychotherapy

Writing about psychotherapy is amazingly like writing about philosophy. It is impossible to define psychotherapy without already implying a point of view about psychotherapy. Any definition immediately contains assumptions, and much of what follows after the definition of psychotherapy is already implicit in the definition. The same age-old problem always arises when one writes about philosophy. With this in mind, let us turn to some basic definitions of psychotherapy and attempt to delineate the rather controversial and amorphous subclass of "psychoanalytically oriented psychotherapy."

Broadly speaking, there are two general forms of the definition of psychotherapy. These are illustrated by the following:

> 1. Whitaker and Malone (1953):
> Regardless of the type or explicit intent of the relationship, whenever one individual engaged in an interpersonal relationship with another functions in such a way as to increase the integrative adaptive capacity of the latter, psychotherapy has taken place.

Therefore, psychotherapy is:
An interpersonal operation in which the total organismic adaptation of one individual is catalyzed by another individual in such a way that the patient's level of adaptative capacity is increased.

2. Wolberg (1954):
Psychotherapy is a form of treatment for problems of an emotional nature in which a trained person deliberately establishes a professional relationship with a patient with the object of removing, modifying, or retarding existing symptoms, of mediating disturbed patterns of behavior, and of promoting positive personality growth and development.

Furthermore:
The relationship, the core of the therapeutic process, is deliberately planned and nurtured by the therapist. Unlike non-professional relationships, which are part of the social nature of man, the therapeutic relationship is started and maintained on a professional level toward specific therapeutic objectives.

Anyone who has read the books quoted above can easily see how the entire theory presented in each book, of what psychotherapy is and how it works, is implicit in these two quite different definitions.

Certain further modifications and specifications emerge from a review of various definitions of psychotherapy, especially those of Shands (1960), Frank (1961), DeWald (1964), Schofield (1964), and Hollender (1965). One may form a subclass of psychotherapy under Whitaker and Malone's definitions quoted above, which can best be termed *psychoanalytically oriented psychotherapy*. This has the following features:

1. It can be defined basically through the terms used by Wolberg in the definition quoted above (please review the definition).

2. It is a private, two-person situation.

3. Its purpose is to foster the acquisition of self knowledge. It is a learning procedure, in which:
The therapist, as the teacher, raises questions which encourage the

scrutiny of certain reactions and he supplies information by pointing out patterns of behavior and the unconscious meaning of communications. As in all important and sustained relationships, learning and change also result from imitation, identification, corrective emotional experiences, and other more or less subtle influences (Hollender 1965).

4. Both transference and resistance are important factors in this learning procedure, although how important they are is a matter of considerable hot debate.

5. There are certain practical arrangements usually followed, such as regularly scheduled sessions of 45 or 50 minutes, a frequency of at least once every two weeks, and the use of a chair either facing toward or at an angle toward the therapist, or of a couch—another debated issue. These arrangements are changed infrequently once settled upon.

6. Hollender (1965) insists the procedure must "depend solely on verbal interchange and non-verbal cues," thus ruling out the use of drugs, physical examination, environmental manipulation, hypnosis, and the like. There is an unreasonableness to this if it is carried to a rigid extreme, and it tells us more about the personality of the therapist than it does about how to do psychotherapy. This rule should be modified to insist that the procedures must depend *primarily* on verbal exchange and nonverbal cues. Relief of severe suffering through the use of drugs is sometimes mandatory if therapy is to take place at all. For example, there are times during psychotherapy when the patient suffers so much that his economic and social adjustment may be threatened—to withhold medication at such times seems unreasonable. Similarly, at the beginning of therapy it may be necessary to help the patients with medication so they can make it down to the office and back without having to be hospitalized. The limits of how long to help and how much to help with medication are often very difficult to decide, but the problem is not solved by rigid refusal *ever* to use medication.

Hollender's (1965) "psychoanalytic psychotherapy" differs from psychoanalytically oriented psychotherapy because, although this term is theoretically presented as "an exploratory, uncovering, cooperative venture," it is not actually used by him with the tone of mutual cooperation and exchange of feelings. In further discussion of the procedure he avoids the questions we are going to focus on in later chapters by setting qualifiers and specifications that seem arbitrary and often unenforceable, such as the refusal to use drugs as mentioned above.

7. There must be motivation; that is, there must be "A sufferer who seeks relief from the healer" (Frank 1961).

8. As to the conduct of the therapist, the basic orientation described by Stone (1961) as "a reasonable human response" or "physicianly vocation," to be discussed in detail later, must prevail throughout the therapy.

9. Just as the patient is learning and developing, the therapist should be learning and developing too. Psychotherapy as investigation or research is a legitimate and scientific way to study human relatedness (Shands 1960).

10. Finally, a most useful division of psychoanalytically oriented psychotherapy as defined above is offered by Gedo (1964). He speaks of (1)"Therapies for current developmental crises" and (2) "Therapies for sequelae of developmental arrest or distortion, including psychoanalysis, supportive therapy, and a heterogenous group of therapies with poorly defined criteria and indications." A shift from one type of therapy to the other within this latter group is possible, but it is not correct or reasonable to assume that only classical psychoanalysis within this group can lead to permanent structural changes within the mental apparatus.

These ten paragraphs hopefully offer a sketchy outline (rather than a rigorous definition) of what might be considered the "boundaries" of psychoanalytically oriented psychotherapy. Wallerstein (1969) has carefully and formally reviewed the categories of issues involved in setting the "boundaries" of psychoanalytically oriented psychotherapy. The rest of this book will offer a detailed exegesis of some of the lesser-known aspects of psychoanalytically oriented psychotherapy in the hope of presenting the "feel" or "ongoing process" of such therapy. The result should be an increasingly clear understanding of what psychoanalytically oriented psychotherapy is and what it is not.

In addition, certain unresolved debates must be clarified in order to understand better some of the issues on the subject that still defy agreement. The first of these, and the most acrimonious, involves the question of whether psychoanalytically oriented psychotherapy can be considered a separate form of psychotherapy at all.

Bromberg (1962) in the preface to his book *The Nature of Psychotherapy,* describes the "lumpers" who seek connections between apparently different things, and the "splitters," who hunt out distinctions and differences between things. Thus certain writers on the subject of psychotherapy, such as Bromberg, Frank, Whittaker, and Malone, are "lumpers" who attempt to describe all psychotherapies as having certain common crucial factors. Other writers, such as DeWald, Waelder, and Gitelson, are "splitters" who cling tenaciously to differentiations in psychotherapy characterized as "pure gold" vs. "copper," and the like.

Wolberg (1954) is a "lumper," who concentrates on the vital elements common to the various schools of psychotherapy. He maintains that if the therapist's personality and technical skills facilitate certain effects, the results of therapy are usually good; otherwise there are poor results regardless of theoretical orientation.

These effects, described by Wolberg as crucial to all successful psychotherapy, are (1) a decent human relationship between patient and doctor; (2) release of feelings with relief of guilt and fear; (3) adjustment to internal or external stress; (4) alteration of defenses destructive to adjustment; and (5) reevaluation of the self with modification of unrealistic attitudes and strivings and substitution for them of productive patterns that lead to more congenial relationships with people.

Frank (1961, 1968) would have us add the presence of the "aura" of the professional expert and the motivation and hope of the suffering person who comes for help as being vital factors common to all successful psychotherapy. Furthermore, the "influencer" must genuinely care about the sufferer's welfare and expend considerable effort to bring about the kind of change he deems desirable.

A much more difficult question is whether there is *anything else* of importance in intensive long-term psychotherapy besides these common factors. The "lumpers" generally feel that the emotional interaction between the patient and the therapist is the crucial factor in all forms of psychotherapy, regardless of theory. This emotional interaction has been called by many names, and focus has been placed on both conscious and unconscious factors in the emotional interaction as being crucial to success.

On the other hand, the "splitters" would, to a greater or lesser degree, distinguish certain forms of psychotherapy, especially psychoanalysis, in which "insight" gained, especially via analysis of the transference neurosis, is the crucial factor and the so-called common factors are either absent or of little importance.

It should be noted that this is not quite logically the same as another debate that rages regarding whether or not there is any clear-cut distinction between "psychoanalytically oriented psychotherapy" and "psychoanalysis," although here again the "lumpers" tend to say "no" and the "splitters" tend to say "yes." Actually there are three overlapping but logically distinct debates that are illustrated by the following diagram (see page 19).

To add to the confusion the lumpers and splitters disagree among themselves as to the extent of their lumping and splitting. For example, Frank (1961) could be described as an extreme lumper with irony and Sargant (1957) as an extreme lumper with malice. To these authors all psychotherapy is characterized mainly by the "suggestion" or "influence" factors, and the rest is of minor importance. Less radical lumpers allow for some differences between the forms of psychotherapy, but emphasize the vital importance of the emotional relationship between doctor and patient. These writers include Whittaker and Malone (1953), Wolberg (1954), Alexander (1956), and Saul (1958).

Wallerstein (1966), on the other hand, characterizes Glover as a radical splitter, differentiating the "pure gold" of psychoanalysis from all other forms of psychotherapy; the latter is portrayed as the "copper" of suggestion. Both Waelder (1960) and Tarachow (1963) come close to this view. On the other hand, DeWald (1964) is a little more modest on the subject, describing a "spectrum" from supportive therapy on the one hand, through "insight therapy" to psychoanalysis on the other hand.

The *ad hominem* argument of the splitters is often present, for example, even in DeWald: "For a variety of motives, many other workers have a more active wish to deny that a significant difference exists between these treatment modalities." These "motives" are further described by Gitelson (1952) as "unanalyzed character defenses" or "countertransference acting out" at least in some cases. It is hard to decide which is the more unscientific, unprofessional, and irritating among some of the writings of supposedly mature psychiatrists—the malice and animosity of the lumpers or the cocky language and *ad hominem* insinuations of the splitters.

Let us now turn our attention to Debate I and Debate II (*Figure 1*). We will discuss them together, since Debate II is a sub-class of Debate I.

The question of whether all psychotherapy is primarily a matter of the emotional relationship between patient and doctor or whether there really is such a thing as a therapy in which gratification through this relationship plays a minor role as compared to the role of "insight" is brought into sharp focus by Searles (1965). It is only reasonable that this should be, since Searles is talking about the psychotherapy of the schizophrenic person—a person characterized by overwhelmingly intense dependent needs often manifested by an insistent and, at times, obnoxious demand for constant immediate gratification. In fact, the schizophrenic, as Searles points out, cannot even conceptualize the idea of psychotherapy on a long-term basis—he sees only the pressing urgency of immediate needs.

This forms an important and immediate practical problem in psychotherapy. Often the patient comes to the first interview asking—even demanding—immediate magical relief. Any attempt to structure or explain the psychotherapeutic process is simply not heard and the patient may not even return; at best he returns with the same demands as if nothing had been discussed at the previous session. Such a patient can turn *anything* in the therapeutic process into gratification of needs. For example, if the therapist is most patient and kindly and explains time after time

Lumpers   vs.   *Splitters*

Debate I.

Certain factors are crucial and common to all forms of intensive long-term psychotherapy.

Forms of intensive long-term psychotherapy can be distinguished on the basis of which factors are crucial to their success.

Debate II.

The emotional interaction, e.g., the "real object relationship" or, e.g., the unconscious interaction between patient and doctor, is crucial in all forms of intensive long-term psychotherapy, regardless of the rituals or theory used.

There are some forms of intensive long-term psychotherapy, e.g., supportive psychotherapy, where the emotional interaction is crucial. There are other forms where it is minor and "insight" is the crucial factor to success.

Debate III.

There is no basic distinction between psychoanalysis and psychoanalytically oriented psychotherapy, as they are both forms of intensive long-term psychotherapy, with common crucial factors.

There is a distinction between the "pure gold" of psychoanalysis and the "copper" of direct suggestion. In psychoanalysis "insight" through interpretation of the transference neurosis is crucial, whereas in "suggestion" —all other psychotherapy— there is merely "education."

Figure 1.

the same basic concepts of psychotherapy, these explanations can be taken as feeding without the slightest insight or understanding. If the therapist tries to do something to bring about relief, such as giving drugs, advice, suggestions, and the like, the patient may greedily accept these and appear at the next session or a few sessions later in the same bad shape as before and demand more magical relief. If the therapist is silent in response to the clamor of all the patient's demands, this can be taken as rejection and the patient does not return.

A certain percentage of these patients eliminate themselves from therapy because no rapport can be established through any alternative the therapist can think of, and they leave treatment convinced that psychiatry is a fraud.

Searles's solution is to refuse as much as possible to directly gratify the patient and instead

> . . . what repeatedly seems to be more helpful to the patient is for me either to encourage him to express his feeling of need as fully as he can, or to convey to him by a brief comment my acknowledgment of his feeling of need, often adding something to the effect that I can see how, under the circumstances, he of course does feel that way.

His major purpose is to free the patient from the guilt surrounding dependency needs, permitting the patient to more readily seek gratification of these needs in his daily life. *His major thesis is that it is incompatible for the therapist to both gratify the needs and help the patient look at the full intensity of the ungratified needs.* Uncovering the guilt and self-hatred attached to these dependency needs is crucial, according to Searles. Then an *ad hominem* argument is added: the therapist trying to gratify the needs "often" is making an unconscious effort to avoid looking at the full intensity of the needs.

The whole problem is immensely complicated by the intense ambivalence in the schizophrenic patient about having his needs gratified. Thus gratification of the schizophrenic can lead to surprising and unpredictable results, depending which side of the ambivalence is predominant.

Yet even the most careful therapist, firmly committed to what Searles calls the "investigative response," cannot avoid giving a "gift" to the patient. This "gift," as Searles points out, is "consistent, attentive, receptive, psychological presence with the patient during the therapeutic hour." In a sense the patient secretly can learn to make gifts out of whatever the therapist is willing to offer, and very often the patient does just that. Everything and anything can be twisted around into the gratification of dependent needs unless the therapist is consciously or unconsciously rejecting the patient, and this is never therapeutic. Discussing whether or not the therapist should directly gratify the patient's needs runs the risk of ignoring the infinite capacity of patients to make out of therapy what they will, in spite of our fancy theoretical orientations and formulations. This is not true, of course, if we are talking about whether or not to give material gratifications such as food or money; it is certainly possible to withhold material gratification although even these the patient can and does use in symbolic fashion.

Does this mean that at least to some extent the debate about gratification versus insight is what has been called (Chessick 1961) a "pseudo problem" in psychiatry? Is it possible that the whole question of gratification is one that is settled by what the therapist is comfortable in giving, and what the patient does with what is given?

Perhaps it is possible to rephrase the problem as follows: Psychotherapy can be practiced in two ways—one style in which the therapist conceives of himself primarily as a *giver* (of drugs, sympathy, advice, education, etc.) and one style in which the therapist conceives of himself primarily as an *investigator.* Those patients who are very guilty about receiving might do better with an *investigator,* where the conscious content of treatment is "research" or "analysis" but the secret wish of the patient is to make use of the interest and attention of the investigator as "gifts." Less guilty patients might use a *giver* directly as a means of keeping going in the face of the enormous demands of life. The guilt in the latter type of patient is also minimized because the therapist's status and wish to give "prove" that it is acceptable for the patient to take. The problem then would become one of finding the best approach for any given patient and then sending the patient to the suitable therapist.

Clinical experience shows that some patients gain nothing by the investigative approach and in fact such patients will shop around until they find a giver whether we like it or not. On the other hand, two kinds of patients do benefit from the investigative approach.

The first kind has already been mentioned. This is the needy patient, sometimes quite intellectual, who must talk "psychoanalyse" in treatment* but who is secretly gratifying himself by the little attentions of the therapist. There is no evidence of the utilization of any of the "insights," although the patient keeps eagerly coming back, for he benefits supportively from the secret gratification.

A great abuse of genuine psychoanalysis when used with such patients can take place here also, for it becomes apparent in a year or two what is going on—the patient has become "addicted" to the procedure (Gitelson 1967). What should then take place is a once-or-twice-a-week psychotherapy with reduced goals, not an interminable analysis, which exhausts the patient's time and money.

The other type of patient who really benefits from the investigative approach gathers and utilizes "insight." This presupposes a sufficient capacity to stand off and observe one's self in a meaningful way. *The best test of "meaningfulness" of insight or "utilization" of insight is whether the patient is actually applying the "insight" to real life and adapting better: is he changing patterns so as to insure more gratification from life and is he showing an increase in emotional maturity as we have defined it?*

How does one determine which style of long-term intensive psychotherapy is best—a primarily giving or a primarily investiga-

* This patient often will insist upon calling treatment "my psychoanalysis" even though coming only once a week and in spite of repeated explanations by the therapist.

tive approach? There is no theoretical formulation and no diagnostic work-up that will formally solve this question. It would seem logical that a definite advantage is gained in always using an investigative approach at the beginning with all patients, including the needy and demanding patient. This is not simply to provide an easier life for the therapist but is in the hope of helping the patient relieve his guilt over his demands so he can then get them satisfied from sources other than the therapist. The aim is to prevent fixation on the supposed omnipotence of the therapist.

However, the decision must be based on a careful determination of the psychodynamics, the anxiety level, and the ego strengths of the patient at any given time in the therapy. A patient with overwhelming guilt about receiving will be made worse by a predominantly giving approach. On the other hand, a patient in a schizophrenic panic or an acute anxiety state is so immersed in emotional chaos that he cannot even hear the therapist's investigative questions. In these situations it seems only common sense that the use of support or drugs or both becomes mandatory.

It is usually possible at the beginning of treatment to recognize those patients for whom an investigative approach *at first* is unreasonable. Depending on whether the patient has a reasonably strong ego that has been overwhelmed by an unusual stress or a very rudimentary ego that cannot tolerate even the smallest stress, a shorter or longer period predominantly of support will be necessary.

The therapist must be able to switch, even during the course of therapy. When the ego becomes overwhelmed by some sudden external event or by a too rapid emergence of repressed material, a temporary relaxation of the investigative approach may be indicated.

The majority of patients, especially nonschizophrenic patients, are not so overwhelmed at the beginning of treatment by such anxiety as would make investigative attitudes unreasonable. In my supervisory experience the giving of drugs at the beginning of psychotherapy has been at times more to relieve the therapist's anxiety rather than that of the patient. Most patients have anxiety at the beginning of treatment; this often disappears as they become familiar with the procedure and the therapist.

My answer to Debate I and Debate II is that for some patients there is more to psychotherapy than simply an emotional relationship. They can and do utilize insight if given enough time to do so. However, it is not possible to predict at the beginning of treatment who those patients will be! Only a trial of therapy for sometimes up to six months will tell the story. In clinical work one is surprised again and again.

The most apparently deteriorated or regressed patient can shift after a suitable period of supportive therapy and begin to utilize insight; the most promising, intelligent, and sophisticated patients can make a mockery out of the therapy.

It is ideal to begin all psychotherapy with primarily an investigative approach if possible, subject to the considerations already mentioned, and then change if necessary. This tailors the therapy to the patient more than trying to fit all patients into a Procrustean bed of any predictive formulation.

It might be argued that at times even six months is not enough time to decide if a patient can utilize insight, and that a shift to a more giving approach is merely a sign of intolerance to frustration in the therapist. It becomes here a matter of judgment, and we must assume that the therapist is healthy enough to make this judgment. If a patient shows no sign whatever in six months of utilizing the predominantly investigative approach, there is little reason to believe he ever will unless a substantial period of either supportive therapy or sometimes just the passage of years takes place, and perhaps not even then. We *must* take into account such things as rigid character armor which simply cannot be pierced, deep early fixations, or severe ego damage.

In making a decision the greatest care should be taken to note the following: (1) Is the patient utilizing the investigative approach primarily as a way of getting secret gratification from the attention and interest of the therapist or are any insights beginning to sink in, as evidenced by their being utilized in life adjustment? (2) Is a transference developing that shows signs of being workable, that is, yielding to interpretation with the consequent development of further insight?

If the approach is being utilized overwhelmingly for gratification, the therapist must consider shifting to a "supportive" or "gratifying" therapy, curtailing frequency of visits to avoid too much regression, and modifying goals. If at least slight transference manifestations are showing, we deal with them in a "psychoanalytically oriented psychotherapy" as defined above, concentrating on derivatives of infantile conflicts.

If deeply regressive, fixed, or fleeting but intense psychotic transference manifestations appear, steps must be taken to reduce the intensity of the transference temporarily by such measures as reduced frequency of sessions and greater supportive activity on the part of the therapist.

Does this discussion throw any light on the other major dispute—Debate III—regarding the difference between psychoanalysis and other forms of psychotherapy? There is general agreement that coming in four or five times a week and lying on the couch does not make a psychoanalysis. What does make a psychoanalysis? Staying strictly with the concept of Freud, we can say that a psychoanalysis is taking place when an investigative therapy is being carried out concentrating predominantly on the resolution of a full-blown transference neurosis that is workable, i.e., one that is resolvable by interpretations with the consequence of new "insight" as proved by changing patterns of living with better adaptation.

The optimal conditions for the development of a workable transference neurosis are believed to be four or five sessions a week lying on the couch, so that if one deliberately sets out to do a "psychoanalysis," this is what he asks the patient to do. However, clinical experience repeatedly demonstrates that a patient can develop a genuine and workable transference neurosis under a variety of conditions. The therapist must follow the lead of the patient and, as Wallerstein (1966) puts it, *go as far as he can go*.

This is not the same as maintaining that all psychotherapy is the same as "psychoanalysis" or even suggesting in any way to attempt by various manipulations to develop a workable transference neurosis in psychotherapy—for such maneuvers often result in an unworkable regressive transference with a stalemate. But there are some patients who, even in psychotherapy once or twice a week, do form a workable transference neurosis and do resolve infantile conflicts through the resolution of these. It is not really possible to predict whether this is going to happen or not without a trial therapy. If a patient is obviously a borderline case, one can be sure that the transference problems will be fleeting (although at times intensive) and regressive and will not yield to interpretation for a very long time.

It follows from the above discussion that there will be patients coming in for years four or five times weekly using the couch who will not be having a psychoanalysis, and there will be patients coming in twice a week who will. The percentage of course would tend to be more for psychoanalysis in patients coming in more frequently, but one should not underestimate the capacity of the human mind to make the best of miserable circumstances or of suboptimal treatment conditions.

The whole problem of what is or is not psychoanalysis has become embroiled in some most unfortunate acrimony and debate. This is illustrated by some of the editorials and papers that have appeared in the *Archives of Neurology and Psychiatry* in recent years (Rado *et al.* 1963; Grinker 1965). It is to be fervently hoped that the various personality clashes involved will recede as the years go by and psychoanalysis will remain as a valuable psychotherapeutic procedure rather than the unassailable property of exclusive and quarreling organizations.

The ideal condition of an investigative therapy would be psychoanalysis, that is, the development and resolution of a transference neurosis with the resulting insight leading to better adaptation. This condition cannot very frequently be met for several reasons. In the first place there are many economic and social factors that preclude patients coming four or five times weekly, and thus the chance of a workable transference neurosis developing is significantly reduced when the frequency of sessions has to be once or twice a week. Secondly, many patients simply do not develop a workable transference neurosis. This is especially true under suboptimal conditions.

When there is not a workable transference neurosis, we must

deal primarily with transference manifestations to whatever extent we deal with transference at all. This is akin to DeWald's definition of psychotherapy. If a full-blown transference neurosis does not develop there can be no resolution of infantile conflicts through direct insight. We deal then only with derivatives of these conflicts in ". . . an attempt to resolve or modify patterns of integration, structural organization and behavior at the level of these derivative conflicts" (DeWald 1964).

However, by arguing that a workable transference neurosis is definitely undesirable in psychotherapy other than classical psychoanalysis the entire problem is being stated backward. Therapy must be tailored to help the patient as much as is possible within the socioeconomic restrictions and the ego capacity of the patient. A workable transference neurosis is *always* desirable in psychotherapy. When it appears, we have conditions for a psychoanalysis; when it does not appear, we have a psychotherapy, and we are forced to be less ambitious in our goals for treatment.

DeWald is undoubtedly correct in pointing out that it is a great danger to attempt to *force* regression in psychotherapy in the erroneous belief that this will lead to a workable transference neurosis. Efforts to force regression lead most commonly to unresolvable stalemate, with intense demands for gratification from the therapist and no insight. Here, of course, lies the danger of the seductive or "smothering" therapist for the patient.

To summarize the chapter, we began with the outline of a definition of "psychoanalytically oriented psychotherapy." We then turned to three important debates raging in the field of psychotherapy today, as outlined in *Figure 1*. Discussion of these debates led to certain conclusions that seem as reasonable as possible, given our present state of knowledge. These are, first, that every psychotherapy ideally should be predominantly investigative in procedure at the beginning. If it appears that the patient cannot tolerate such investigation or if he only utilizes the investigation as gratification for dependent needs without any insight even after six months, it is often best to modify goals and switch to a more tangibly giving supportive therapy. Otherwise the therapy can be continued as a genuine psychoanalytically oriented psychotherapy.

If this leads to the development of a full-blown transference neurosis resolvable by interpretation with consequent insight, we have the basic conditions for a psychoanalysis regardless of the rituals of the treatment. If not, we have a psychoanalytically oriented psychotherapy dealing mainly with derivatives of the infantile conflicts.

This approach hopefully tailors the therapy to suit the needs of the patient in a maximal fashion and reduces the tendency to force the patient into the therapist's preconceived notions of what the therapy is to be like. It also increases the possibility that suitable patients who are prevented from coming in four or five times weekly for reasonable economic or social factors can still obtain maximum possible benefits from psychoanalytically oriented psychotherapy.

4

Supportive Therapy

Before examining the process of psychoanalytically oriented psychotherapy in detail, it is necessary to digress and to define "supportive therapy" or the "giving approach" as we have used it in the previous chapter. It should already be clear that "supportive therapy" does *not* mean directly giving material gratification to the patient except in the most unusual circumstances.

These circumstances do arise occasionally in certain emergency situations in which the patient doesn't have carfare home, must be helped out of jail, and the like, and has no one else to turn to, or in acute situations, in which the patient can only "respond to primary process" (Eissler 1952).

Almost exclusively, however, support basically means functioning as an accessory ego for the patient—"being of use" as Hill (1955) puts it. It is hoped that gradually the healthier attitudes and capacities of the therapist for dealing with problems will be introjected by the patient (Giovacchini 1965, 1967) leading to increased ego strength in the patient.

The concept of "ego strength" and methods of assessing ego strength in a patient are used here in a practical sense, implying capacities for functioning and adaptation in everyday life. DeWald

(1964) discusses this in detail and the reader is referred to his clear discussions of the "general" and "specific" aspects of "ego strength." DeWald points out:

> The more an individual has had a general pattern of persistent effort in a goal-directed fashion, and of success in the various ventures that he has undertaken, the more likely will he be to sustain his effort during the course of the treatment, and ultimately to achieve some measure of success.

The patient's capacity for sustained object relations, his motivation, intelligence, psychological-mindedness, types of defenses, age, and life situation all must be taken into account in assessing whether therapy should or should not be geared primarily to supportive goals.

In borderline and schizophrenic patients who are suffering from massive anxiety it may be necessary to "be of use" to the patient for a very long time before conditions are reasonably calm so that the patient can look at what is inside himself. Classic neurotic patients, on the other hand, may need very little of this. An introjection of the nonanxious and benevolent attitude of the therapist is a vital part of reducing massive anxiety that is often associated with severe preoedipal longings, but it often must be combined with "being of use" in little ways such as advice giving, support, and the like. It is hoped that the distinction between being of use in little ways and massively involving one's self in the care and feeding of another person is obvious.

There is not much debate about what constitutes the essence of support in psychotherapy, although Wallerstein (1969) points out that the procedures are not clearly delineated or agreed upon. The elements are:

1. Reduction of anxiety by various techniques such as administration of drugs, attention, and selected gratifying of dependent needs. Even the careful taking of a history with a medical aura

about it can be quite gratifying and supportive for the patient.

2. Permitting the patient to discharge emotions in a nonpunitive situation and in a nonjudgmental situation.

3. As Alexander (1965) writes,". . . objectively reviewing the patient's acute stress situation and assisting his judgment, which is temporarily impaired under the influence of severe emotional tensions . . . ." Such objective review of the situation and of goals in life is always supportive and valuable even if the situation is not one of acute stress. It provides the conscious and rational aspect of the "consolation of philosophy."

4. Modification of superego and ego functions by conscious or unconscious identification with the therapist. For example, this is often the essence of therapy with adolescents. Growth through various partial identifications is characteristic of this stage of life. The therapist consciously and deliberately presents himself as a model by his behavior and by describing his ways of dealing with serious matters. The patient identifies with this model, which results (hopefully) in healthier ways of behavior and dealing with problems that result in greater life success for the patient. This stimulates the patient to further identification.

5. Support of neurotic defenses in order to prevent the outbreak of psychosis. The importance of this is self-evident.

6. Manipulation of the environment. In my opinion this is a *highly over-rated* supportive measure, which ignores the amazing power of the repetition compulsion. Time and again therapists have attempted to manipulate the environment either directly or through social agencies, only to be frustrated by the difficulty of so doing, or frustrated by the patient's capacity to either undermine the manipulation or to go from the frying pan into the fire.This is especially true in attempts to manipulate marital situations. The therapist must be very careful to avoid playing God regardless of how horrible the marriage seems to be. If a patient is in a bad marital situation, there is a reason that he is there; the need for men and women to get into mutual torture situations sanctified by the term "marriage" seems to be extraordinarily widespread. All sorts of rationalizations can be given for staying in these situations, the most common of which are the "children's welfare" and "religion" excuses. Actually the children are often

much better off when some of these marriages are broken up, and religious leaders of all faiths are taking an increasingly enlightened view of what constitutes a worthwhile marriage in the theological sense.

In general, manipulation of the environment is of value mostly in therapy of children and adolescents, and should be used for adults only when there is a *very* clear-cut alternative to the patient's present situation that is capable of being followed and seems definitely better.

The real debate involving "support" as described above is whether this is or is not the essence of all psychotherapy. There does seem to be an increasing consensus that support is essential and unavoidable in all forms of psychotherapy. Most psychoanalysts seem to feel that support, although present in their kind of psychotherapy, is of minor importance compared to the insight gained through analysis of the transference neurosis. It is of course impossible to prove, but my impression is that a great deal more supportive therapy goes on at certain crucial moments in the offices of all but the most doctrinaire psychoanalysts than is generally acknowledged.

In stressful situations the physicianly vocation of the psychotherapist is and should be depended upon, and the impact of this is extremely powerful. A compassionate gesture from Frieda Fromm-Reichmann (1950) or an impatient foot-stamping by Sigmund Freud left a very deep imprint on the patient indeed.

Most psychoanalytically oriented psychotherapy contains a combination of support and attempts at gaining insight; both elements are of great value. The therapist attempts to permit the patient to go as far as he can go in the development of a transference neurosis but often he has to be satisfied to deal with derivatives of the nuclear infantile conflicts in combination with giving support or transference gratification (to be discussed in the next chapter) as needed. The limitations of therapy arise out of the limitations in the capacity of the patient's ego, as previously discussed, and also often out of limitations on either the patient's financial capacity or time available for treatment sessions.

PART II

Technical Aspects

5

Transference and Transference Neurosis

This long chapter defines and reviews certain generally accepted basic procedures and processes that are fundamental to psychoanalytically oriented psychotherapy. These are known as transference, transference neurosis, transference resistance, and gratification in the transference. Although all these processes are involved in all therapies, they are separated somewhat here for purposes of presentation. The discussion attempts to concentrate on the controversial aspects of these processes and procedures, with reference to texts that adequately describe the generally accepted aspects.

Running throughout the discussion is the thematic question of how to set a balance in psychoanalytically oriented psychotherapy between investigation and gratification in the transference. In the style of a Henry James novel, we will look at this question again and again from different points of view as it comes up in the various contexts of all the procedures and processes that constitute psychoanalytically oriented psychotherapy.

There is almost universal agreement on the crucial importance of the transference in psychoanalytically oriented psychotherapy but far from unanimous agreement on how this concept is to be understood and still less on how transference is to be "dealt with" in treatment. The classic review of the subject up to 1954 is given by Orr (1954). The basic definition of transference is given by Fenichel (1945):

> The patient misunderstands the present in terms of the past; and then instead of remembering the past, he strives, without recognizing the nature of his action, to relive the past and to live it more satisfactorily than he did in his childhood. He "transfers" the past attitudes to the present.

Fundamentally, transference is a form of resistance in which the patient defends himself against remembering and discussing his infantile conflicts by reliving them, but it also offers a unique opportunity to observe the past directly, and thereby to understand the development of the conflict.

The development of the transference and the "handling" of the transference account for some of the most difficult problems in doing psychotherapy. For example, there is an attempt in psychoanalysis, according to DeWald (1964), to develop a "full-blown regressive transference neurosis." He writes, "The development, exploration and ultimate resolution of the transference neurosis becomes the central theme of the analysis. . . ."

In actual practice, we see all varieties of transference developing, whether one is doing psychoanalysis or psychoanalytically oriented psychotherapy. A deeply regressive transference neurosis can appear in the first session, a situation we consider ominous, usually indicative of schizophrenia. No clearly noticeable transference reaction may appear over long periods of psychotherapy. Transference phenomena may be consistent and fixed to the point where no amount of "handling" or interpretation seem to budge the transference at all, or transference phenomena may change wildly from day to day, even though the transference is very intense or very deeply regressive at any given time. This is illustrated in the following diagram:

Parameters to Describe
Transference Phenomena

Notably absent	Notably present and very intense
Fleeting and changeable, unpredictable from day to day	Fixed and unchanged by manipulation or interpretation
Manifestations mainly derivatives of infantile conflicts	Deeply regressive wishes directly felt and expressed

Figure 2.

Using terms such as transference neurosis and transference psychosis is very confusing unless the terms are carefully defined. One may define them as phenomena depending on insight as well as intensity. Thus a transference psychosis is an intense transference, which may or may not be fleeting, and is utterly without insight on the part of the patient. A transference psychosis is not useful in psychoanalysis or psychotherapy.

Psychoanalysis tries to foster a situation in which the transference is intense, relatively consistent, and deeply regressive; a situation is called the "transference neurosis" when the analyst is the major object of this kind of transference. Somewhat paradoxically, Glover (1955) points out that the "transference neurosis" may pass unnoticed! This important paradox is recognized by Glover, and he answers it by contrasting the "classical" case with the "not so classical" case in which the transference neurosis does not obviously and automatically develop.

This line of reasoning is carried further by Tower (1956) in a most remarkable and candid paper. She considers the term "transference neurosis" a misnomer:

> . . . in view of what actually occurs in an analysis. In general,
> the transference phenomena are experienced in multiple and
> varying forms throughout any analytic experience, and by
> both patient and therapist. A discrete, well-structured easily
> describable transference neurosis as such probably seldom
> occurs. . . .

The quotation from Tower can be applied to psychoanalytically oriented psychotherapy with considerably less disagreement
being evoked. Whether a classical transference neurosis really occurs more frequently in the standard psychoanalytic situation is
highly debatable; there is no scientific evidence on either side of
such a debate.

Giovacchini (1965) offers a useful approach to these verbal
confusions in his definition of "transference neurosis." He begins
by reminding us of the classic concept of transference neurosis as
meaning the projection of infantile feelings *exclusively* onto the
analyst, a situation that probably never occurs! His modification is
to consider ". . . the transference neurosis . . . as a focal object
relationship which for the moment may supersede all other object
relations." The crucial issue is whether the transference neurosis
as so defined can be resolved—if so it is a "therapeutically workable transference or an operable transference."

The word "resolved" as used here is very tricky. We assume
it to mean a dissolution through the process of appropriately timed
interpretations. We further assume that proof of such a desirable
kind of resolution would be an increase in the patient's insight and
utilization of this knowledge for better adaptation and emotional
maturity.

In fostering the development of a workable transference, both
Giovacchini (1965) and Stone (1961) emphasize the importance of
the analyst's attitude and behavior. Successful "resolution" or "dissolution" or "minimization" (Stone) of the transference neurosis
as defined above is *the* unquestionable cornerstone of psychoanalysis as a therapy.

To what extent is this true in psychoanalytically oriented psychotherapy?

If the previous discussions have been clear, the answer to this question follows logically. There are two forms of psychoanalytically oriented psychotherapy with respect to the question of transference neurosis. In those cases where no clear-cut transference neurosis appears, the question of resolution is meaningless. To whatever extent transference appears in such psychotherapy, it is used as a tool to gain insight on a level of derivatives of infantile nuclear conflicts. Deep interpretations of infantile nuclear conflicts on the basis of low intensity nonfocal-object (Giovacchini) transference manifestations constitute *wild analysis* and lead only to fixed resistances.

In those cases of psychoanalytically oriented psychotherapy in which a genuine transference neurosis appears, as already discussed in Chapter 3, DeWald is not correct to complain about this appearance as undesirable, complicating, and disrupting of treatment. His complaint fits better the appearance of a transference psychosis as defined above, and certainly every effort must be made to prohibit transference psychosis and to break it up if it occurs.

However, *a genuine transference neurosis does occur with considerable frequency in psychoanalytically oriented psychotherapy, especially in the therapy of borderline cases, and will require dealing with pregenital infantile nuclear conflicts whether the therapist likes it or not. Attempting to break this up by manipulation is experienced by the patient as rejection by the therapist, based on the therapist's fear of the patient's magically charged pregenital strivings.*

It is scientifically impossible to *prove* whether the patient improves in the psychotherapy situation because (1) he gains insight through correct interpretation of the transference neurosis or (2) he experiences the interpretations and the "physicianly vocation" attitude (Stone) of the therapist as "gifts" and gains transference gratification—or because of both of these factors. The major intellectual effort is toward proper recognition and interpretation of the transference neurosis; we assume that the therapist is sufficiently emotionally healthy so that the traits of "warmth, decency, reliability, kindness and integrity" (Stone) will appear naturally and without effort.

A large proportion of patients who enter psychoanalytically oriented psychotherapy are not suffering from the classical neuroses but are either schizophrenics or, even more frequently, members of that vast group of borderline* patients who are sometimes diagnosed as "character disorders" and sometimes as "borderline schizophrenia," or the like.

When transference phenomena begin to appear in such patients, there is bound to be an appearance of intensive and preoedipal longings and conflicts of every kind and description. The tendency of the inexperienced or incorrectly trained therapist is to avoid confrontation with and involvement in the patient's intense and massive preoedipal longings, since these obviously stir up deeply repressed similar longings long since buried in the past of the therapist.

There seem to be two characteristic ways that incorrectly trained or inexperienced therapists use to avoid confrontations with and to avoid becoming deeply involved in the patient's intensive and massive preoedipal longings. In the first way, he will break up the transference neurosis by refusing to interpret, reducing the hours, or even getting rid of the patient on the basis of various rationalizations and theoretical arguments. In the second way, he will attempt to minister directly to the patient's needs in an effort to reduce the intensity of those needs. The purpose of this is to decrease the intensity of the confrontation with intense needs from the patient, and also, due to an overidentification with the patient, the therapist is really ministering to a projected part of himself.

Breaking up the transference neurosis is the easier of the two ways to observe, and also easier to find arguments and rationalizations to justify it, but it can have disastrous effects, as the following brief case history illustrates:

* In the present text the term "borderline schizophrenic" or "borderline patient" will be used interchangeably to refer to this group of patients.

Mr. L. T. was a 45-year-old artistic and talented individual, who was struggling with a vast inner emptiness. He had a schizophrenic-like episode at the age of 24 upon finishing college, which he resolved without professional help by marriage to a rigid and commanding woman much like his father. The episode was characterized mainly by unbearable feelings of loneliness and restlessness with inability to function, but no overt schizophrenic symptomatology. He drifted around the United States and Mexico for a few months until meeting his wife and marrying her. He then returned to Chicago and settled down to help his father in business. Mother was a schizoid individual who spent her time cleaning the house. Besides his wife and his father, both of whom were stern and strict people, but who did show an interest in the patient, he developed a close relationship with a kindly elderly couple who were next-door neighbors, and kept himself busy for over ten years with work and artistic activities. Only his lack of any other social relationships indicated that something was wrong.

Then the elderly neighbors moved away and the underpinnings of the patient's solution began to fall apart. His wife had become more domineering as she got older and she was preoccupied with ordering their five children about. The old longing and restlessness returned.

He began to drink and to stay up into the wee hours of the morning, pacing the floor and making telephone calls. He wrote love notes to the office secretary, but never culminated anything with her. She borrowed (and never repaid) a substantial sum of money from him. The painful restlessness became so apparent that he appeared strange socially—he could not sit still or carry on a conversation. In this state he entered treatment with me five years ago.

There were many telephone calls at two and three in the morning; the patient could not even sit in the waiting room before his sessions and had to pace up and down in the hall until it was his time. He resembled a patient with akatizia except he was not on phenothiazines. The focus of his emptiness gradually turned on me, although the bulk of the psychotherapy at two sessions weekly was based on a strategy of support and encouragement to return to previous modes of adjustment such as his artistic activities. He settled down and was able to continue working. Finally he developed an affair with a female artist, which represented an acting out of his transference longings toward me, enabling him to avoid the direct pain and the homosexual aspects of such longings, which were extremely intense and most primitive (see the discussion of transference in borderline patients in Chapter 12).

With this safety valve it was possible to begin very cautious interpretations of his infantile longings, which we discussed as the need for a "blue fairy" (good breast) and all this entailed. I brought in the magic from *Pinocchio* and the opening scene of *Babbitt*— the dream material was filled with such portrayals—and we worked deeper and deeper toward a frank recognition of these longings and toward exploring avenues of gratification that were possible. The patient began trying some new things and reviving old hobbies and interests.

After four years, I had to transfer this patient to another therapist as I was leaving the city for a considerable period. Having been involved in the training of this therapist, I knew that he had twice failed to complete his own personal treatment, with the situation floundering both times when intense transference longings threatened to develop. I hoped, nevertheless, that the situation would work out since the patient was well along in insight.

What I did not foresee, however, was that not long after I left the city, the house of the female artist burned down and as a result she left the area. The patient was then left utterly alone with the new therapist. He made a colossal effort to deal with the problem by focusing on the new therapist and developing new interests, such as home gardening.

The new therapist did not recognize what was happening. He spent most of the sessions discussing the new interests on a superficial level, attempting to maintain a "supportive relationship." There were no interpretations. The patient began feeling that the sessions were being wasted and asked to reduce frequency, which the therapist agreed to genially and without exploration or interpretation.

The patient began to be flooded with great rage at his father and at his brothers. The therapist dealt only with the superficial reasons for the rage and was unable to recognize the deep feelings of rejection in the patient. Finally, after loading up on alcohol and barbiturates, the patient put a bullet in his gun, put the gun to his head, and pulled the trigger. The new therapist considered this playing "Russian roulette" and saw it as merely an attention-getting device. Fortunately the gun was old and did not go off.

By this time I had returned to the city. The patient called me one day at 5:00 A.M. and asked to see me. He was rapidly calmed down at this first session by the simple device of retaking his complete history and, in a sense, starting over again with me. He was so angry at the previous therapist he canceled all appointments with him before we even had a chance to discuss it.

This case provides an excellent illustration of a number of the points previously discussed. The patient entered therapy and in spite of an initial and justifiable strategy of supportive therapy he developed an operable transference neurosis, although he needed to bring a third person into the transference (the female artist) so that the situation could be bearable.

It must of course be pointed out that the need for acting out the transference neurosis with the third person because of the unbearable pressure of the pregenital longings—so typical in borderline patients (see Chapter 12)—clearly prevented a psychoanalysis, since the ego could not tolerate the transference neurosis at that point. However, the patient was on his way to eventually working through this acting out in psychoanalytically oriented psychotherapy.

The new therapist was in the unfortunate situation of receiving the full brunt of the transference longings when the third person moved away. His own emotional difficulties made it impossible for him to recognize what was going on; he had to stay on the pleasant surface and avoid experiencing the unbearably painful emptiness of this patient, even empathically, even for a moment, even when the patient tried to kill himself. The strategy of decreasing frequency of sessions—which on the surface might seem logical to avoid the development of a transference neurosis—was really based on the therapist's fear of a regressive transference neurosis, as described by Searles (1965). If anything, the sessions should have been *increased* in frequency at this point. It would have been necessary to interpret the empty feelings of the patient and help him as before, but to recognize this would have required an empathic feeling in the therapist as to what was going on. This was missing.

Here is a very difficult case of a borderline patient in psychotherapy with an operable transference neurosis, which, if patiently and properly "handled," leads to definitive therapeutic gain.

The second way of avoiding the transference neurosis, ministering directly to the patient's needs in a massive fashion, will be discussed after we turn to the concept of "transference resistance."

No discussion of transference and transference neurosis is complete without a discussion of the phenomenon of transference resistance. This can really be quite confusing in terminology. Upon review of Fenichel's classic definition of transference given earlier, it is clear that all transference is a form of resistance, that is, resistance to remembering. The patient attempts to relive and to reexperience without remembering.

Thus the appearance of transference manifestations at a point in therapy where unconscious material is preparing to emerge into awareness can be thought of as a "transference resistance." It substitutes for the unconscious material and also changes the focus of the material being discussed.

There are two situations in which transference becomes a fixed form of resistance, often leading to a serious impasse in psychotherapy. The first of these occurs when the patient repeatedly rejects all suggestions that his feeling or behavior in a certain situation is "transference" at all. Assuming that it *is* transference, and not a reaction to something in the therapist that the therapist is unaware of, this can lead to a very difficult situation.

For example, I treated a patient who alternated between episodes of depression and hypomania. She was extremely ambivalent in all her relationships, and similarly toward me she consistently emphasized one side of the ambivalence—an enormously grasping, swallowing, and engulfing attitude and behavior.

At worst it was a cannibalistic incorporative demeanor that she presented to me hour after hour.

There was also a consistent minor key of insults and derogatory behavior toward me; at times there were wild explosions of fury at the psychiatrist who was treating her sister and at doctors "in general." Yet the patient absolutely denied any but the most ingratiating and positive warm feelings for me. Repeated interpretations of her comments and behavior were met with bland denial or "It must be there if you say so."

This was clearly a form of psychotic denial, for whenever this patient became even dimly aware of her unbelievably furious rage at her mother she was overwhelmed with guilt and went into a hypomanic or depressed episode. The patient was protecting herself from a depression—which she experienced as the most horrible kind of punishment for her—by resolutely refusing to recognize the negative side of the ambivalence toward me and subsequently toward the mother. She used a similar isolation technique in dealing with her anger toward her mother in therapy—she knew the rage was there and admitted it must be, and yet she could not *feel* it. To have felt the rage toward me in the transference would have been a definitive step toward feeling the rage at mother, with all the magic consequences of the loss of the mother through cannibalistic incorporation.

The problem of this kind of transference as a fixed form of resistance, therefore, becomes the problem of dealing with psychotic denial in psychotherapy. One hopes that as the relationship with the patient becomes sufficiently strong, the patient can drop such defenses and feel enough security to work through the problem.

The second situation in which transference becomes a fixed form of resistance occurs when the patient insists on continuously trying to gain gratification in the transference.

In all supportive therapy there is a gratification offered to the patient of his unconscious transference wishes and needs. Some of this, to a relatively lesser extent, is going on even in the most investigative forms of treatment. The situation of "transference resistance" comes up most clearly in psychoanalytically oriented psychotherapy when, as the transference manifestations emerge in the treatment, the patient becomes increasingly fixed on getting these transference needs gratified by the therapist, and refuses to look elsewhere. The therapy becomes stalemated by the patient's insistence that nothing else is any longer important except obtaining gratification of the newly emerged desires from the therapist.

DeWald (1964) sees this situation, which he calls "transference resistance," as arising, for example, when an overly ambitious psychotherapist tries to do a psychoanalysis in face-to-face psychotherapy. Two ways to avoid this are given by DeWald:

(1) Insist on relative abstinence regarding drive-derivative gratification in insight-directed therapy. "Gratifying the transference wishes tends to intensify this 'transference resistance,' and gives support to the fantasy of ultimate transference gratification."

(2) Confront the patient with the existence of the transference resistance and suggest that he look elsewhere for gratification, using "conscious repudiation" and "sublimation."

We are now in a postion to discuss whether gratification of the transference wishes ever makes sense, and if so what form of gratification is of value. Let us begin by returning to the second way of avoiding the transference neurosis mentioned above, as illustrated by the neophyte therapist trying to minister directly to the patient's needs in order to escape from involvement in the preoedipal longings of the patient as they are appearing in the developing transference neurosis. Here is a form of gratification in the transference that does not make sense.

A deliberate attempt, out of theoretical preconceptions, to provide direct massive transference gratification to patients leads to further regression and infantilization of the transference with increased magical dependent expectation from the therapist. Such maneuvers—which are suprisingly common, especially among inexperienced therapists—may constitute a form of acting out by the therapist. The unconscious motivation, as it has appeared in my supervisory experience with neophytes, is an attempt by the inexperienced therapist to avoid being faced with the deep intensity of the pregenital longings of the patient—which stir up similar yearnings in the therapist.

From the preceding discussion it can be seen that what is being unconsciously attempted by the therapist is to convert the transference neurosis into a transference resistance, stalemating the therapy, and stopping the development of more and deeper transference phenomena.

Even more extreme examples can be cited of therapists avoiding interpretations and directly attempting to minister to patients' needs by providing "tender loving care" and the like. This can result in some pretty extreme acting out by the therapist—occasionally even crossing the boundaries of professional propriety. More seriously, such behavior tends to fix the patient on magical expectations from the therapist, which are sooner or later bound to be disappointed. Many patients have such omnipotent expectations from the therapist anyway, which must be eventually uncovered and understood for what they mean in terms of infantile longings and conflicts. However, if the therapist attempts to play a directly omnipotent role, such uncovering can never occur and eventually an explosion may result with the *serious danger* of suicide.

On the other hand, we have already pointed out that some forms of gratification in the transference seem to go on whether the therapist likes it or not. Assuming that the therapist is not going to make massive direct efforts to minister to the patient's needs, what kind of gratification should take place, and should the therapist ever deliberately provide or change the level of this gratification?

Hill (1955) stresses the fact that at least schizophrenic patients bring the "transference resistance" (again defined as attempting to get gratification in the transference) into the psychotherapy *regardless* of the skill or wishes of the psychotherapist. Perhaps following Hill's attitude of "willingness to be of use" fosters the transference resistance too. The main point is that many patients move rapidly into the phase of a full-blown regressive transference neurosis in psychotherapy with intense wishes for gratification in the tranference whether the therapist likes it or not! This is especially true of schizophrenic patients, and borderline schizophrenic patients. As Hill describes it:

> The underlying drive in the patient is to find in the therapist an all-satisfying and satisfied provider of all the supplies he needs and an understanding protector who, without tension, or anxiety, or anger, will happily remove from the patient all sources of discomfort, frustration, anxiety, or anger. The drive is to force the therapist to be a good breast, uncluttered by any disturbing attributes.

How is this to be broken up? Hill proposes to supply the patient with "moments of good relationship," which, although they are a poor substitute for what is wanted, are better than anything he has had before. This leads to modification of the transference resistance, for the patient takes in the "goodness" like mother's milk, and grows. That is to say, usefulness, goodness, understanding, clarification, and other healthy qualities in the doctor lead to an increase in the patient's ego strength by introjection, with a consequent movement away from the transference resistance.

The glue that holds patient and therapist together through thick and thin of psychotherapy over the years of time is the mutual gratification in the transference-countertransference structure (to be discussed later). From the patient's (unconscious) point of view it is gratification in the transference that keeps him coming. However, the skilled therapist knows—usually intuitively—just the right amount of gratification in the transference that the patient should have. If there is too much, the patient does not grow but focuses on getting more gratification. If there is too little, the patient experiences too much anxiety and pain and, unless the patient is masochistic and thus giving him pain is really giving him gratification in the transference (!), the patient will fall apart or leave therapy, usually the latter.

The optimal level of gratification leaves the patient with some anxiety—just enough to drive him to master the situation by finding new techniques of adaptation in the external world.

The greater the ego strength, the more the patient is able to utilize interpretations of what is going on in the transference in his striving for mastery; the less the ego strength the more the patient has to find some form of gratification before the anxiety level from malevolent introjects is sufficiently reduced so he can begin to seek mastery of his problems.

As to the crucial question of *what kind* of gratification in the transference is to take place, this is a function of both the therapist and the patient. A large part of the nature of this gratification depends on what the therapist is comfortable doing and on the relative ages and sexes of the therapist and patient. As strange as it may sound, there is not so much difference between the elderly lady therapist serving tea and cookies in her home office and the eager young man therapist taking an enthusiastic and sincere investigative approach to the patient. The patient can easily experience both as gratification.

The basic assumption is that the therapist is not acting out countertransference problems in such a way as to use the patient as a means of secret satisfaction. It is hard to believe, for example, that a young male therapist should ever engage in any kind of contact of a physical nature with a young female patient, although this has been done in a variety of ways with a variety of rationalizations. The feelings aroused in the therapist in such a situation would have to lead to immensely complicated problems, even if they were controlled. *More fundamentally, the therapist must know himself and be honest with himself; there must be adequate rest and time for self-scrutiny with every patient or these situations inevitably arise.* Consultation with an experienced colleague is the most valuable safety valve available.

Therefore a *rigid* distinction between kinds of gratification in the transference—for example, symbolic vs. material or intellectual vs. physical—is unnecessary and confusing. The purpose of withholding gratification in the transference is to achieve an optimal anxiety level that will drive the patient to seek better adaptation to external reality so as to achieve more gratification elsewhere, and to avoid a "transference resistance" in which the patient becomes fixed on the therapist's supposed omnipotence. It is the *anxiety level* that must be kept in mind in deciding how much to gratify, *not* either (1) an attempt to meet the theoretical ideal of being "neutral" since this is impossible or (2) a theoretical fear of the patient developing a fixed transference resistance— which is really a fear of the patient's needs being dumped on the therapist.

One provides or withdraws gratification in the transference to charge the therapeutic atmosphere with just the proper incentive to further work; sometimes this means reduction of frequency of sessions and even temporary interruption of treatment. If the therapist is not embroiled in his own countertransference this can be an important and effective technique. It assumes the capacity to empathize with the patient's anxiety state and need state at any given time.

When a patient persists in attempting to gain gratification in the transference and refuses to turn anywhere else, I believe this to be a function of either something wrong in the therapist or a sign of a psychotic transference as we have defined it.

In summary, we have first defined the terms transference, transference neurosis, and transference psychosis. A tranference neurosis can occur in psychoanalytically oriented psychotherapy, and is not to be feared if it develops spontaneously. Beginners tend to respond incorrectly to a transference neurosis in psychoanalytically oriented psychotherapy by either breaking up the therapy or attempting to directly gratify the intense needs expressed. The former is experienced by the patient as severe rejection; the latter tends to fix the patient on the supposed omnipotence of the therapist.

The term "transference resistance" is a rather confusing one, since all transference represents resistance to remembering. It can be used to indicate the appearance of transference manifestations when repressed material is about to emerge, thus changing the focus of the therapy away from this material. Or it can be used to stalemate the therapy, either by a psychotic denial that clear-cut transference manifestations are transference at all, or by fixation on getting gratification in the transference rather than understanding the transference itself.

Gratification of drive derivatives as they appear in the transference is useful within limits in those situations in which anxiety becomes intolerable and the patient cannot function, threatening both the therapy and the patient's life situation. The skillful therapist, both by good timing of interpretations and by knowing when to allow some gratification in the transference, keeps anxiety at an optimal level for therapeutic progress.

6

Interpretation and Insight

As a prelude to the discussion of interpretation, it is worthwhile to remind the reader of Saul's (1958) discussion of "understanding unconscious material," since obviously all interpretations must be based on the understanding of such material. He begins by advising us to keep very close to the "material" of free associations produced by the patient and not to introduce our own associations. It is important to look for big major central themes first —the "red thread," as Saul calls it—and to attempt to distinguish and focus upon the underlying dynamics of the patient derived from the surface content of the associations given by the patient. He writes:

> No matter how unintelligible the associations or the dream may be, at least the main topics and tendencies, the emotional forces and something of their interplay, are usually discernible. . . .

It is necessary, in listening to what the patient reports, to separate present life situations, transference, and childhood patterns, as well as to remember to think of the possible occurrence of major current stimuli in the patient's life. Saul believes that repressed impulses emerge more and more frankly as associations progress (and as a dream progresses). It is important to identify those associations connected with the greatest emotional response and to search out progressive as well as regressive forces in the patient, and to determine where the patient is in terms of his object relations, identifications, projections, and sense of self.

The two most useful recent textbooks that contain pointers of value in the practice of psychoanalytically oriented psychotherapy existing today are those by DeWald (1964) and Saul (1958). The sections in these books on "interpretation" are well worth reviewing for a standard discussion of the subject. We will not attempt to cover the same material, but will concentrate on the controversial issues.

"Insight," or knowledge of one's own personality operations, is usually spoken of in psychotherapy as being "intellectual" or "emotional," but there is considerable confusion on the subject (Brady 1967). The common usage is that if the patient can mouth new information gained about himself in suitable terminology, but makes little use of this information, he has "intellectual" insight. This undesirable situation tends to come about in two ways. First, when interpretations are made before a patient is "ready" for them, the interpretation may be accepted for a variety of reasons but is useless to the patient. He parrots the interpretation back on command but does not utilize it in changing his adaptational techniques. Second, it comes about as a general part of the patient's use of intellectualization as a defense. This is especially true of obsessional and certain superintellectual types who are warding off a schizophrenic reaction. They may be loaded with intellectual insight about themselves—some of which may be true, but which is useless to them. Intellectualization with isolation and repression of the affect are the defenses involved. Interpretations of any kind are usually useless with such patients before a great deal of preliminary gratification in the transference.

Insight may come as primarily an intellectual or primarily a sudden or emotional experience in therapy. How it comes is not as important as how it is used.

If it is used in a meaningful way in changing life patterns —"emotional insight"—it is of prime value. Therefore, to see if an interpretation has led to useful insight one watches the reaction of the patient to the interpretation and follows the utilization that is made of the interpretation in changing life adjustment. A "correct" or meaningful interpretation is often responded to with some show of affect or with further corroborative material, memories, and dreams. Sometimes it is responded to with negative affect, or with a delayed response appearing a session or two later. The ultimate test of "insight" is utilization toward accomplishing the aims of psychotherapy, as defined previously, to increase adaptative capacity.

An interpretation can be viewed as a source of information or as an emotional experience itself. The latter view is less common, but Frank (1961) points out that even when it is presented in the most noncommittal terms, an interpretation reveals information about the competence of the therapist and his attitudes. A good interpretation—whether it is exact or inexact—increases the faith of the patient in the therapist, and thereby reduces anxiety and heightens a sense of security. Simultaneously it reassures the therapist as to his own competence—leading to the well-known phenomenon of neophyte therapists bombarding the patient with interpretations of the fanciest kind in order to reassure themselves of their own competence.

Furthermore, patients may utilize interpretations in the most spectacular manner in the transference. For example, one patient insisted that every interpretation made to her was a harsh criticism. This was not paranoid, for the content of the interpretation was not distorted but rather the *concept* of interpretation itself invariably came across as being a harsh, sadistic, and critical attack to this patient—much as her mother had constantly attacked her. It was impossible for the patient to conceive of a comment of any kind coming from an authority figure as anything but harsh, sadistic criticism.

An example from the opposite extreme comes from a psychotic patient who had started therapy with a psychoanalyst. The analyst was very quiet and very sparing in comments and interpretations. After about twenty sessions the patient changed therapists. She could not stand the tension of so much silence, although the approach being used was technically correct. I talked, chattered, and interpreted to her whenever I could for several months. The patient utilized this as a straight feeding situation, which she simply had to have first, and gradually gained strength so that after a year we were doing essentially the same thing she found unbearable with the first therapist.

An interpretation may be thought of as "exact" or "inexact" (Glover) or "partial" or "total" (Alexander). It may also be thought of as well-timed or ill-timed, as right or wrong, and as a reasonable fit or simply wild. Interpretations may be of content or of resistance, and it is generally accepted technique to interpret resistance first. I will not discuss the subject of "resistance" formally in this book since it has been thoroughly and meticulously reviewed recently by Greenson (1968), and the chapter on this subject in his book should be studied by every psychotherapist. Alexander (1956) writes:

> Interpretations which connect the actual life situation with past experiences and with the transference situation—since the latter is always the axis around which such connections can best be made—are called total interpretations. The more that interpretations approximate this principle of totality, the more they fulfill their double purpose; they accelerate the assimilation of new material by the ego and mobilize further unconscious material.

This seems to be an incontestable statement, but one rarely realized in the practice of psychotherapy. Most interpretations are not total, although if at all possible we would like them to be.

Tact, phrasing, and correct timing are matters quite difficult to teach. Perhaps the best teachers here are the patients' reactions to our mistakes. If one is willing to learn from one's patients there should be a steady improvement in tact, phrasing, and timing as one gains in experience. At the beginning, identifications with the techniques of one's therapist, teachers, and supervisors are usually the starting point, but gradually an individual "style" emerges.

Special attention should be paid to the problem of dream interpretation, which is a subject surprisingly neglected in the literature on psychotherapy. There is not much agreement on how dreams should be "handled" in psychotherapy. Some therapists avoid them altogether; others seem to be so fascinated by them that their patients feed them endless strings of dreams. The decision of what to do with a patient's dreams in psychotherapy must be tailored to the patient and the nature of the treatment situation; there can be no easy generalizations on this subject. (The same is true regarding the use of interpretations the therapist *knows* to be inexact, as will be discussed later.)

We must start from the fact that some patients bring in very few dreams and some bring in many dreams indeed. The general tendency is to focus more on the dreams when they occur few and far between and to focus away from them when they are in abundance.

One should always ask the patient to tell one or two of his dreams and for his earliest memories at the beginning of every psychotherapy; it is part of the initial history. Taken together with carefully assembled historical material, the initial dreams and the earliest memories should almost always enable one to construct an initial "genetic-dynamic" formulation of the patient. This is formulated as a hypothesis in one's mind and is of infinitely more value in treatment than a "diagnosis." One should not, as Saul seems inclined to do, interpret this initial genetic-dynamic picture to the patient, for such a procedure comes across as too godlike and too magical, and it also encourages overintellectualization.

In the therapist's mind, when the patient presents dreams, he should try (after eliciting the usual associational material) to fit the dreams into the genetic-dynamic formulation he has already made and, if necessary, alter this formulation. In discussion with the patient, however, he should try to concentrate on the relationship of the dream to the focus of what is being discussed in the therapy at present, and to keep dream interpretation *in that focus and on that level.* It is mandatory to avoid clichés and symbols and always to speak the patient's language, not textbook language.

Let us take, for example, the dream of a borderline patient with paranoid tendencies. The patient entered therapy because of an irrational anger at her sister-in-law, who is a dogmatic person but has not acutally done anything to justify the intensity of the patient's hatred of her. The patient knows this and presents it as the reason for treatment. Patient's mother is a cold, harsh, and domineering person and father has been repeatedly institutionalized for episodes of schizophrenia; surprisingly, there are definite warmer early memories involving father but not mother. In fact there is much material that could be foolishly interpreted as "oedipal" in this patient; this material actually represents a longing for a bit of warmth wherever she could get it. Patient married a rather domineering and insensitive man who puts up with her paranoid tendencies and occasionally flares up and bawls her out.

After several months of treatment the patient is focusing on her marital problem and her need for warmth from her husband; at the same time she feels how difficult it is to get a warm response from him. Part of this is in the patient's own personality—she is so suspicious that it is hard to warm up to her. Since any other transference manifestations are covered up by this suspiciousness, any "total" interpretations so far have been impossible. Only resistance, in the form of suspiciousness and mistrust, could be interpreted.

A dream fragment is presented:

I am at a dinner party seated between my sister-in-law and my mother-in-law. I feel quite trapped. Mother-in-law is a good cook, but sister-in-law is taking the credit for her cooking. It is a nasty situation.

One might make a mental note of the oral and homosexual elements in this dream, as well as the defensive mechanisms of denial and displacement. This fits previous formulations about the patient. In terms of dealing with the patient, however, I chose the feeling of being "trapped" to discuss. It was the predominant feeling in the dream, and led to a tremendous release of feelings about her husband and the marriage. It opened up a discussion of the patient's contribution to the "trap" that she felt her marriage was, which was a step forward for this patient.

The principle followed here was to try to relate the dream material to the focus of therapy at the time of the dream, and to deal with the dream in terms of the material of the therapy, even though this means neglecting important deeper elements for some future date. The shakier the ego structure of the patient, the more valuable this technique becomes, for obviously these very shaky patients cannot tolerate further rapid uncovering in any beneficial manner.

This approach differs from classical psychoanalytic dream interpretation in that only certain aspects of certain dreams are chosen for study by both doctor and patient, and other aspects are deliberately neglected. Thus the therapist is more active and selective, which undoubtedly influences the material produced. It is a matter of argument whether in psychoanalysis the exact same thing does not go on anyway, except in a more subtle fashion. There is no body of evidence conclusively for or against this contention.

An excellent and useful review of classical psychoanalytic dream interpretation has appeared, written by Altman (1969), and filled with valuable clinical insight. Even in the most strict psychoanalysis, Altman correctly observes that:

> In clinical practice, our choice of interpretation is based on the context in which the dream is given. When we single out one element from among many, we select according to the relative weight and balance of the contents of the patient's mind, preconscious as against unconscious, past against present, defense against drive. We select for emphasis that which will have the most meaning for the patient at the moment.

In psychotherapy the same approach is correct to an even more highly selective degree, and also influenced by the lower frequency of sessions with less available time.

Finally, the importance of the inexact interpretation should be underlined. Properly used, this provides the patient with intellecutal defenses against material he cannot handle, and as such is an important part of supportive psychotherapy. The price of offering inexact interpretations is that, if uncovering psychotherapy is attempted later, it will run into fierce resistances and complications.

Improperly used, as it most often is, the inexact interpretation is simply the wrong interpretation made by a therapist who is convinced he is right. It *is* possible to jam an interpretation down a patient's throat either through argument or through more subtle rewards that may be offered if the patient is a "good" patient, accepts the interpretation, and makes "progress"—thus reassuring the therapist of his skill and of the correctness of his theory. The price of this is the same—further uncovering at a later date becomes immensely complicated.

For example, a patient was admitted to the hospital after a suicide attempt. She had been in treatment with a psychologist in the area who was trained at a psychoanalytic institute (not in the area) and called himself a psychoanalyst. He had her coming five days a week and working at three jobs to pay his fee. She was a single girl and had no money left over for much except room and board, as she was an unskilled clerical worker. He gave many interpretations, which she swallowed eagerly, in the expectation that soon she would be happy and no longer depressed. She was on the couch and produced a flood of dreams and free associations for him, which were duly interpreted. After two years of this the patient began losing hope more and more. Her resentment began to increase tremendously at the unfulfillment of rewards she had fantasied were waiting for her after she gained enough "insight." Finally, when the "psychoanalyst" announced he was going away for a five-week vacation to an expensive resort area, the patient brought a bottle of acid into his office and attempted to drink it in his presence. He panicked and called the police, who brought her into the hospital.

The patient was found to be a borderline schizophrenic with tremendous feelings of emptiness and hopelessness. Therapy had to be geared strictly to reality-testing and getting her to return to work and use her money for some realistic satisfactions; such a network of intellectualizations had been constructed that no uncovering work was possible at all. It was judged too dangerous to break down the faith that the patient still had in what she had "purchased" from the "psychoanalyst" with her hard-earned money, as it seemed to be all that kept her from an overwhelming emptiness and psychotic collapse. So this was left alone and support was given to help the patient get what she could from life and reduce her expectations of eventual total solutions to her problems with consequent (oral) bliss.

This kind of situation arises quite frequently in many contexts, in which the inexact interpretations are gobbled up and weaved into a form of oral gratification by the patient, the case subsequently breaking down in a year or two when the patient realizes gradually that there has been no change in his actual life situation. The eager accumulation of the interpretations, although they were useful as a form of gratification, were not enough to neutralize the deep emptiness of the patient and were not utilized in actually changing the patient's adaptative techniques so she could meet her needs from life itself. Here again it is incumbent on the therapist to keep a continual and careful watch on what the patient is doing with the interpretations. As previously discussed, some patients are never able to utilize interpretations, and are eventually best treated by a less frequent supportive therapy with limited goals.

Let us turn now to the even more complex and less understood aspects of therapy in an attempt to delineate and describe certain vital sets of processes that actually all go on simultaneously and are crucial to healing by psychoanalytically oriented psychotherapy.

7

Working Through

The fact that "working through" has to take place in psychotherapy is evidence on the side of those who minimize the importance of "insight." For strictly speaking, if insight were—as it was once believed—the mainstay of psychic change, then when it was achieved there would promptly be change. However, experience has shown that usually there has to be a period of substantial length between the time of insight and evidence of genuine psychic change. Brady (1967) writes:

> In any case, most writers agree that insight usually only sets the stage for significant clinical improvement. Time is required to translate the newly acquired perceptions and attitudes into more healthy patterns of behavior.

It must be conceded, therefore, that even in the strictest psychoanalysis there is a long working-through period of intense interaction between patient and therapist. This may be characterized as necessary to achieve complete or integrated insight into all facets of the patient's problems or alternatively as necessary to achieve "emotional" insight, or in still another way as a corrective or educational experience for the patient. At any rate it is considered at an end when the patient shows definite evidence of utilizing his insights to improve his adaptational capacities.

Strictly for the purpose of clarity of presentation a very important distinction will be drawn between "working through" and "after-education." This is an artificial distinction in that both take place simultaneously, but it is most advantageous to discuss them separately. For our purposes "working through" is conceptualized as a cerebral or intellectual process that must take place before a presented insight can be actually utilized in producing a change in adaptive behavior. It is generally accepted clinical knowledge that a variable period is required between the presentation of insight and its actual utilization by the patient. The processes that must go on during this period are defined as "working through."

"After-education," on the other hand, is conceptualized as a more general set between mainly emotional conscious and unconscious processes that go on between the patient and the therapist, with an important effect on the maturation of the patient. This involves such controversial issues as "corrective emotional experience" on a conscious level or "symbolic core experience" on an unconscious level. Classical psychoanalytic therapists tend to look with disfavor on after-education, although the concept was introduced by Freud. We will not discuss after-education further in this section (see Chapter Nine).

We shall examine three descriptions of the working-through process, given by Shands, DeWald, and Marmor, in order to illustrate important differences in conceptions of working through, which may be combined to give a more complete understanding of the process.

Shands (1960) takes an approach to psychotherapy that might be called a "research approach." His orientation toward the whole matter is especially valuable for those interested in research on the process of psychotherapy. He views this process basically as one of "changing descriptions." The situation is designed:

> . . . to facilitate data processing into patterns of description, both in terms of an examination of previously undescribed aspects of the series of events and in terms of the alternative description from a different point of view.

The mechanisms of defense are for the purpose of maintaining familiar ways of processing data, for the processing of data in a novel way tends to be experienced as unpleasant. The end process of working through has been found when the therapist and patient agree substantially on their descriptions. Thus the patient ". . . ceases to be a patient when he consistently formulates his experience in agreement with the therapist."

Shands is very much oriented toward philosophy. He points out the analogy of psychotherapy to "war games," for in psychotherapy there is a preparation for the combat of living. This "game" phenomenon lies in the simultaneous participation with another person and observation of the event, where a relationship takes place and yet there is an artificiality to the situation. When the patient is "prepared" by the process of working through, his descriptions of events are quite similar to those of the therapist and he is ready for real living.

It should be noted that a closely analogous situation has been described by the difficult and controversial philosopher Wittgenstein, who succeeded the famous G. E. Moore in the professorship at Cambridge in 1939.

After his death, Wittgenstein's *Philosophical Investigations* (1955) was published and in it he substantially revises his views of 1921 as presented in his only previously published work, *Tractatus Logico-Philosophicus* (Wittgenstein 1953). *Philosophical Investigations* is an almost unreadable muddle of aphoristic writings collected and rearranged over many years by the author. Careful study reveals certain basic and very important themes in the work. These are:

1. The speaking of language is in itself a form of life. The actual use of language is like a game, let us say like chess. It has certain

rules that must be observed by those who play the game, and there are certain restrictions on the moves that are allowed. Since we use language in a multiplicity of ways, we speak of each of these ways as a "language game."

2. "Our language can be seen as an ancient city: a maze of little streets and squares, of old and new houses, and of houses with additions from various periods; and this surrounded by a multitude of new boroughs with straight regular streets and uniform houses."

3. Language is much more complex than previously believed, and is used in a variety of related ways. "Language games" form a "family" in that when we look for similarities between the various "language games" we "see a complicated network of similarities, overlapping and criss-crossing. . . ."

4. Bertrand Russell (1959) explains Wittgenstein: "Thus by learning to play a variety of language games, we acquire the meaning of words through and in their use. . . . The raising of metaphysical problems would then be the result of a defective grasp of the 'grammar' of words".

Philosophy, for Wittgenstein, would consist of clearing up confusions in our use of language. If we could obtain complete clarity in our use of language, it follows that philosophy would disappear, for philosophical questions only arise when we "don't know our way about" in linguistic usage.

5. There is a philosophical prejudice in favor of the "primacy of the private," that is, first we have private experiences and then we label them with words. Words can be behavior. For example, adults can teach a child new pain-behavior so that the verbal expression of pain *replaces* such primitive expressions of pain as crying, rather than *describing* pain. This is further brilliant demonstration of the enormous complexity of the use of language and the variety of language games.

6. Thus language is learned as a series of language games, many of which have important utility and are *instruments* for various purposes. As Levi (1959) puts it:

This is to pass far beyond a theory of meaning which identifies meaning with the connotation and denotation of names. The significance of an expression is like the *power* and the *functions* of a knight or rook in chess; to understand the piece you must understand its utility for the game. It follows that there are plural pieces with plural utilities.

An aside is now in order to the reader regarding the complexity and difficulty of this material. He may be asking, "Why can't this subject be made more clear and simple?" The lack of a "clear and simple" presentation of "*the* rules" of language ("*the* language game") is not a function of poor writing; it is because of the fact of the multiplicity of language games. The search for one clear and simple set of rules is responsible for serious and hopeless paradoxes in philosophy. This is the basic and brilliant contribution of Wittgenstein.

Furthermore, the use of "games" in Shands and Wittgenstein should not be confused with the best-selling *Games People Play* (Berne 1964). In this latter superficial text the games are played so as to get something from someone else. A series of rather typical situations between people are described as "games" and given an importance out of proportion to their value as consistent patterns in people's lives. Thus identifying and shifting these games is fun and can produce superficial changes, but since basic patterns of neurotic repetition are not being touched, no basic changes can come about.

The games of Shands and Wittgenstein, on the other hand, are played internally and arise not out of the deliberate effort to get something from somebody but out of a conditioning process established in very early childhood. In fact, these games develop in such an early and basic way that they become our way of perception of the external world, and our way of speaking; they underlie and at the same time affect and restrict our perception and language.

We are now in a position to focus in greater depth on the

views of Shands. First of all, he points out the remarkable fact that in spite of much conscious disagreement among the so-called schools of psychotherapy, there is "a surprisingly wide area of *unconscious* operational agreement upon method and attitude." This is because "It is characteristic of human beings not only to have a language but also to be intolerant of the language of their neighbors."

The therapist from any given school of psychotherapy presents certain interpretations in the language of his school. Shands calls this a *description* (of a series of events from a certain point of view). The obvious question arises as to how one knows which descriptions are true and which are false. This brings us at once to the analogy with Wittgenstein.

For a description is like a language game. Just as there is no one "true" language game, with one set of "true" rules, there is no one "true" description. Psychotherapy is ". . . an intensive training in the use of words to contain and convey the universe." It is completed when the descriptions of the patient are in substantial agreement with the descriptions of the therapist. To put it in another way:

> The psychotherapeutic situation comes to an end when the descriptions of the two participants are reasonably similar. The patient in the psychotherapeutic situation becomes free of the situation when he has accepted it. In the usual terms, we say that he has "worked through his resistances"; that is, he has ceased to resist. He ceases to be a patient when he consistently formulates his experience in agreement with the therapist.

If the process of psychotherapy is one of changing descriptions, does this not open it to both the malicious criticism of Sargant (1957) and the friendly criticism of Frank (1961) that it represents simply a "brainwashing" or resembles a religious or political conversion? Is there any justification for changing the descriptions of the patient or is the therapist just doing this to produce another adherent to his "school" of thought?

We as psychotherapists must answer this question, and it is not really hard to do if one has followed the discussion so far. If therapy is undertaken to make an adherent to the "one true school" of thought, then it is no different from religious conversion. If, however, it is undertaken as a medical procedure to improve the adaptational capacity of a person, then the problem is resolved. We are trying to provide the patient with a better instrument to adapt to the demands of the external world and the demands and restrictions coming from internal drives, conscience, and the like. The test of therapy, therefore, becomes a test of whether the patient's adaptation or emotional maturity has improved. Borrowing from Fromm (1955), we look for evidence for an increase in the patient's capacity for reasoning, loving, and productive working.

Thus, changing the descriptions of the patient so that they come into substantial agreement with the descriptions of the therapist improves the patient's adaptational capacity, for the descriptions of the therapist are better power instruments—that is, they explain and predict more accurately and consistently. The question then becomes not one of the "truth" of a given description set, but of its adaptational value. The various schools of psychiatry represent a variety of description sets which have been found to have considerable adaptational value as power instruments and so have attracted adherents. To search for the single absolutely "true" description set is futile and impossible.

The parallel between this approach and the philosophy of Wittgenstein is even deeper. Descriptions, just like language games, have a multiplicity of uses. Sometimes these uses conflict, and one must sacrifice the use of a language game or description for one purpose in order to use it for another purpose in a given situation. An excellent example is what Sullivan (1953) calls the "paranoid crystallization," in a marvelously accurate portrayal of the development of the paranoid delusional system. Unbearable anxiety is reduced by the paranoid crystallization, which is a description set as defined above and adopted for that specific purpose. Unfortunately, however, in adopting a paranoid description set, one must sacrifice alternative description sets that would have much greater power as instruments for adaptation. The result is the paranoid patient sitting on the back ward of the state hospital in a totally unadapted state but clinging tenaciously to his description set for the purpose of reducing unbearable anxiety.

Similarly, although the various schools of psychiatry do not have to undergo a "truth" test in the classical philosophical sense of "certainty" or "truth," they do have to undergo a test of usefulness. As the years go by, those schools of therapy that provide the descriptions that show power to improve adaptational capacity will undoubtedly gain predominance, and other schools, which may have temporary periods of fashion, will decline.

In addition there is an economic factor involved. Those schools providing the maximum adaptational gain in the minimum amount of time with the minimum expense will tend to predominate. Unless it can be demonstrated over the years that lengthy and expensive procedures provide the patient with substantially more adaptational capacity than relatively shorter procedures, the former will also tend to disappear.

As schools with less adaptational value go into eclipse they will take on more and more the characteristics of a group of religious fanatics with a firm core of devout and orthodox believers holding out against the slightest change in doctrine.

The best example of this in our present day is the Jungian school of psychoanalysis. This group has faded to a certain hard core that will buy any published books on Jungian theories and Jungian psychoanalysis, and they continue to hold the line on Jung's rather esoteric and mystical doctrines. Such a small core will probably exist for many years, long after Jung's description set has been superseded by much more powerful and economical description sets.

To follow Wittgenstein further, let us review his notion of the task of philosophy, which is to clear up confusion over language games. When we have "lost our way about" in language games, philosophical problems arise. The classic example of this is the question of "truth" or "certainty." Wittgenstein was much influenced by the theorem of Goedel that demonstrated the existence of true but *unprovable* propositions in the *Principia Mathematica* of Whitehead and Russell. Similarly, to find our way about the various schools of psychiatry we need a sort of metapsychiatry, which should form the basis of psychiatric research (see Chapter Fourteen).

It is of paramount importance to have a clear conception of those questions which can and cannot be answered, so as to avoid debate and rancor over unprovable propositions. Of even more importance is to recognize that certain questions, such as how to ascertain the absolute "truth" of a psychological description set, are illegitimate and rest on a confusion of language.

Since the term "working through" was first elucidated by Freud (1914), the reader may wonder why this discussion did not begin with the classic psychoanalytic conception of the term. The reason is that, as complicated as Shands' description of this procedure may be, it is both a clear and operational presentation and may be grasped with a little careful thought.

Turning on the other hand to the psychoanalytic conceptions, one is surprised by several matters. In the first place, although there is increasing agreement on the importance of the working-through process in psychological healing, corresponding simply to a diminishing emphasis on the curative power of uncovering unconscious ideation, there is an astonishing lack of publications on the subject. This is true in spite of Freud's (1914) conclusion that ". . . it is a part of the work which effects the greatest changes in the patient. . . ." In the second place, those scattered publications that exist are in wide disagreement. In general there is a more classic approach to working through characterized by descriptions in metapsychological terminology (Karush 1967), and a more unorthodox approach characterized by use of learning theory. We shall examine both of these approaches.

DeWald (1964) presents a classic approach with a minimum burden of metapsychological terminology. He sees working through as a broad process involving (1) an oscillation in the patient between "getting worse" and "getting better" and (2) repeated presentation of certain formulations in varied and interesting ways, by the therapist. In addition to this it is vital for the patient to attempt to modify and change himself or his situation; equally vital are the therapist's responses to these attempts.

The implications in this brief description are tremendous, but in DeWald, as in most texts on psychoanalysis or psychoanalytically oriented psychotherapy, they are not explored or developed to any great extent. A great area of controversy and confusion in the field of psychotherapy lies in the question of the relative importance of the formal analysis of the transference neurosis and of the working-through procedures. Perhaps because psychoanalysis was historically founded on formal analysis of the transference neurosis there has been a tendency to emphasize this and to slide over the working through. A more orthodox explanation might be that in psychoanalysis the analysis of the transference neurosis is conceived of as the crucial element and working through is a minor theme, whereas in psychotherapy the reverse seems to be true.

DeWald devotes a whole long chapter to transference and only a few pages to working through; if one wishes to look deeper one must read the book backward! That is to say the notion of the "getting-better"–"getting-worse" oscillation is explained in an earlier chapter without being referred to as working through; it is mentioned as the crux of working through in the pages on the subject, without being explained.

At any rate, according to DeWald, besides "breathing spells" for "consolidation" (undefined) of process of insight and awareness,

> The process of insight-directed psychotherapy thus involves the intermittent mobilization of conflicts and anxiety in amounts that are tolerable and will not overwhelm the patient. This is followed by interpretations of content, designed to help the patient's conscious ego integrate the quantum of the previously unconscious conflict. This produces a repetitive cycle in which the patient temporarily "feels worse," followed by conscious ego resolution or integration and "feeling better" again.

In more detail, we begin by interpreting resistances and defenses. This tends to mobilize unconscious conflicts; in addition the "therapist's attitude" leads to regression and also mobilizes these unconscious conflicts. Such mobilization leads to anxiety and the patient "feels worse." Then the content of the conflict is interpreted, allowing the ego to further integrate the now conscious material, and the patient "feels better." We then revert to the original procedure, and so on.

As to the interaction between the patient who is attempting to change himself and his situation and the therapist who is observing and—hopefully—responding to these attempts, no further details are given, except that the therapist should support the patient's effort to change. It is apparent that in DeWald's presentation the conditioning aspects of working through are kept at a minimum emphasis.

Before focusing on conditioning, let us continue discussion of the classical approach to working through, well reviewed in detail in a paper by Novey (1962). Freud recognized the *time lag* invariably attendant upon the assimilation of correct interpretations during which certain vital but poorly understood processes take place. This *time lag* is most difficult to explain. That it hopefully leads to the "assimilation" of interpretations and their consequent use in changing adaptational patterns seems generally agreed, but *how* it leads to this remains debatable.

Fenichel's (1945) views are quite advanced on the subject of working through. His explanation of the time lag is borrowed from Rado, who compares working through to the work of mourning, an unquestionably unfortunate and confusing comparison, as demonstrated by Stewart (1963). "Working through" is characterized by Fenichel as

... demonstrating again and again the unconscious impulse, once it has been recognized, in its manifold forms and connections, and in attaining thereby the cessation of the pathogenic defense.

The long duration of psychoanalysis is accounted for by

> . . . the education of the ego to tolerate less and less distorted derivatives, until the pathogenic defense is undone.

Fenichel insists that any procedure that works by undoing resistances and interpreting transferences may be called psychoanalysis and especially that there is no difference based on whether the patient lies down or sits, or other rituals of procedure. After a relatively short period of time, by empathic listening to the free associations, by careful history-taking and by eliciting dreams and memories of the patient, the astute therapist can form some pretty good ideas of the resistances and conflicts that the patient has. A certain time lag takes place from the time the therapist begins interpreting resistances and conflicts to the time they are "assimilated," that is, made use of by the patient in changing himself or his situation.

The procedure differs from indoctrination in that the therapist stays conscientiously with the patient's material and empathically resonates with the patient's unconscious. He is then able to interpret the patient's unconscious accurately and is not presenting his own preconceptions *de novo* to the patient. But, for a genuine assimilation of interpretations to occur, a very complex process goes on between therapist and patient that takes a substantial duration of time.

No discussion of the classic approach to working through is complete without a metapsychological description. The most accepted is based on Freud's (1926) formulation that not only must the ego's repressive forces be overcome but there is a magnetic force called "id resistance" that *pulls* unwanted ideas into the unconscious. Thus the time lag between insight and "assimilation" of insight is due to the necessity of overcoming the ego's repressive forces *and* "id resistance." Stewart (1963) contends very reasonably that this is an "unclear" and "somewhat mystical" formulation, and accounts for the poor understanding of working through. He feels that Freud deliberately left the matter open so further clinical experience could enrich the concepts and permit their further elaboration.

Working through does not consist in either simply a tailoring of descriptions to fit those of the therapist or in an oscillation in states of greater or lesser anxiety as a consequence of interpretations. It contains an additional vital element, an educational experience in which the therapist, whether he likes it or not, conditions the patient.

. The conditioning process in working through is a vital, although rather neglected, aspect of the operation. A variety of recent authors have looked at the subject quite differently, straying from the orthodox and introducing learning theory concepts to varying degrees. There seems to be a fear among some of these authors that psychoanalysis will turn out to be simply a form of conditioning or even worse, indoctrination. This fear is unfounded. Those who accuse psychoanalysis of being simply conditioning or indoctrination are poorly informed and are throwing out the baby with the bath. On the other hand those who refuse to see that the therapist influences or conditions his patient are more interested in preserving separateness of technique and status than in knowing what they are doing.

The even more complex emotional interaction between patient and therapist, as previously stated, should not be classified as part of working through, although it provides the motivation for the therapist and patient to work through together. Thus it has been proposed in this text to restrict the definition of working through to a series of intellectual operations that go on between patient and therapist during the time lag between interpretations and assimilation of interpretations.

These intellectual working-through operations would therefore be (1) the fitting of descriptive sets between therapist and patient, thus providing the patient with a better power instrument for adaptation; (2) the classic operations of interpretation of resistances and content with subsequent widening and deepening of insight; and (3) a subtle conditioning procedure that influences the patient's thought and behavior.

A more detailed exploration of this conditioning procedure is presented by Marmor in a series of papers (1964, 1966). He differentiates "cognitive learning," "imitation" (identification with the analyst), and a "subtle conditioning procedure" as major factors in the psychotherapeutic process.

There is not much more to be said about imitation, or identification with the therapist, as far as working through is concerned. It is so well known as to be the subject of many jokes. Every therapist willing to look for it has observed it.

The subtle conditioning, on the other hand, has only recently come to the attention of psychotherapists. There is an astonishing ignorance on the part of the psychiatric profession about the theories and findings on the learning process produced primarily by psychologists. In most residencies the neophyte psychiatrist is carefully made familiar with a large variety of similar and unimportant drugs and left without special emphasis on the conditioning effect of the therapist's attitude on the efficacy of the drug (Chessick and McFarland 1963). In a similar way, there is no training on how a patient learns from a therapist, and in what the most effective teaching procedures might be. The net result is that conditioning in most uncovering psychotherapy goes on in a haphazard fashion, and both therapist and patient are sometimes a little ashamed of being made aware that is going on at all.

If we face the fact that we *always* are conditioning the thought and behavior of our patients whether we like it or not, it becomes vital to examine the ways in which this can be done and to attempt to bring it under more conscious scrutiny. The most vital feature, of effective conditioning, according to many research findings, is the intermittent approval of the therapist when he is pleased coupled with withholding of approval—not punishment—when the therapist is displeased. This very typical interaction, which goes on both at a verbal and nonverbal level, is indispensable for all conditioning to take place.

Focus on the importance of conditioning would of course explain Marmor's and Shands' contention that good results in psychotherapy are less dependent on the theoretical inclination of the therapist than they are on his personal characteristics, emotional maturity, empathic capacity, and clinical experience. So far all available evidence supports this contention.

Furthermore, to make matters even more complicated, the nonverbal aspects of this subtle conditioning are the most important. The use, for example, of the "mm-hmms" of a therapist to manipulate the content of the so-called "spontaneous" productions of a patient has been experimentally demonstrated (Marmor 1964). There is a most lamentable paucity of studies of this nature, which are quite important for a better understanding of working through.

Perhaps the most mysterious and fascinating of all the nonverbal conditioning in psychotherapy has been pursued by Nacht (1962, 1963). The "deep inner attitude" of the psychoanalyst or psychotherapist produces a major reconditioning effect on the patient. It functions to reduce the patient's fear of closeness, bit by bit. It is difficult to describe this operation to those who have not experienced it, but in principle it represents still another form of subtle conditioning, although far less amenable to scientific investigation and certainly a most insufficiently investigated phenomenon.

Carrying the application of learning theory even further, Marmor questions the whole concept of transference. He suggests that the frustrations of the psychoanalytic technique, if they don't lead to breaking off treatment, lead to a characteristic regression seen in prolonged frustrating situations, to more primitive behavior. We call this the "transference neurosis" when it occurs in the psychoanalytic situation.

He concludes:

> Although this so-called re-activation of the "infantile neurosis" is considered to be an essential aspect of classical analysis and an important desideratum, it is by no means a proven fact that this is either the only or the best route to the eventual establishment of more mature patterns of behavior.

This formulation suggests the rather extreme viewpoint in which the transference neurosis itself becomes the by-product of the working-through process—a by-product of questionable value!

It is possible that all three of the major operational processes described above—fitting of descriptive sets, repeated interpretation, and subtle conditioning of thought and behavior—work concomitantly to overcome both the ego's repressive forces and the id resistance we are struggling with. There is no reason why these operations could not be further studied and characterized in metapsychological terms, so that a more harmonious fusion could result. Undoubtedly a greater understanding of the working-through processes could lead to a greater effectiveness in psychotherapy. This will indeed be a task for the experts, and hopefully will afford a long overdue meeting point between psychoanalytic theorists and experimental psychologists.

8

The Optimal Working Alliance and the Countertransference

The Optimal Working Alliance–The importance of the working alliance conceived of as a separate phenomenon from the transference neurosis was not sufficiently stressed until recently. If there is a proper therapeutic atmosphere, as defined by DeWald (1964) and Stone (1961), the conditions are good for an optimal working alliance to form. This atmosphere is provided by the personality of the therapist and his office accoutrements and routines (which are an extension of the personality of the therapist [Greenson and Wexler 1969]). Through his personality and office setting and routines the therapist demonstrates to the patient his integrity, sincere therapeutic intent, willingness to work hard and seriously for the patient's benefit, and perhaps above all his genuine respect for the patient as a human being. This is condensed by Stone into the phrase "physicianly vocation" of the therapist.

If the therapist's personality does not possess these qualities, there is no way the patients can be fooled. Most patients are experts in detecting phonies and double-message communications, and the most careful therapist will betray himself in one way or another. This is obviously true of long-term therapy in which patient and therapist are together frequently over months and even years.

It is this repeated contact, one to four hours weekly for years, that builds up powerful feelings between two people—powerful enough to have an impact that changes them both. The nature of this interaction, taking place over *years* of time, has not been sufficiently understood. One facet is clear, however: if the personality of the therapist is such that he cannot provide a therapeutic atmosphere for his patients, then no basic changes can be made in the mental health of the patient. If the patient does not leave treatment, either occasionally a flight into health or usually a stalemate that punishes both parties is the result. This is true whether the therapy is a formal psychoanalysis or uncovering psychotherapy, regardless of the theoretical orientation of the therapist, regardless of how intelligent and perceptive the therapist is, and regardless of how much training and experience he has had. Greenson (1965) gives some splendid examples of this in his discussion of "aberrations" of the working alliance.

In Chapter 10 we will discuss the factors in the personality of the therapist that interfere with empathy in psychotherapy. These are the same features that make a therapeutic atmosphere impossible. Very briefly, these factors are anxiety in the therapist for whatever reason; unanalyzed narcissism in the therapist; unmet needs of the therapist in his personal life, including lack of adequate sleep, leisure, and vacation; a tendency to slip into bureaucratic routines and traditional rituals, vanity, and greed.

If a therapeutic atmosphere cannot be provided, there is little hope for a successful psychotherapy. Is it true that if a therapeutic atmosphere is provided, an optimal working alliance will develop? The answer to this question is, unfortunately, no.

Greenson (1965) points out that some patients, by the nature of their pathology, are incapable of forming a working alliance. He writes:

> The actual alliance is formed essentially between the patient's reasonable ego and the analyst's analyzing ego. The medium

that makes this possible is the patient's partial identification with the analyst's approach as he attempts to understand the patient's behavior.

However, those patients who cannot split off a reasonable observing ego will not be able to maintain a working alliance. Or to put it another way, the ego must be able to operate in such a way that two dangers are avoided. These are (1) regression without any insight, and (2) clinging to a rigid relationship without daring to even temporarily or partially regress. The patient, writes Greenson:

> . . . must be able to communicate in a variety of ways; in words, with feelings, and yet restrain his actions. He must be able to express himself in words, intelligible with order and logic, give information when indicated and also be able to regress partially and do some amount of free association. He must be able to listen to the analyst, comprehend, reflect, mull over, and introspect. To some degree he also must remember, observe himself, fantasy, and report. This is only a partial list of ego functions that play a role in the patient's capacity to establish and maintain a working alliance. . . .

It is possible to *train* the patient's ego in the therapy situation to the point where the working alliance can be formed, maintained, and improved. This is done primarily, as Greenson points out, by focusing on the alliance in such a way as to reinforce those ego functions that are contributing to it and to stimulate more optimally the necessary ego functions that are inadequate. A "mutual concern" with the working alliance tends to enhance it.

Therefore, to have an optimal working alliance there must be a therapeutic atmosphere, a patient with ego functions capable of forming a working alliance, and continual concern with the state of the alliance. This is not all, however. Buried in the quotation from Greenson above is the phrase "and yet restrain his actions," which is not elucidated by him. The optimal working alliance also depends on the inhibition of both "acting-out" and of "acting-in." Tendencies toward such behavior must be restrained and understood both by the patient and the therapist. This is based on the conviction that acting-out and acting-in are both substitutes for verbal communication, remembering, and observing, three of the most vital ego functions necessary for a working alliance to develop and be maintained.

The phrase "acting-in" was introduced by Zeligs (1957) with the help of Rangell. It represents

> . . . a middle phase in a genetic continuum in which acting out, *without verbalizing or remembering*, is at one end—acting in lying somewhere in between—and verbalizing and remembering *without action* is at the other end.

It is not the place here to go into the highly controversial and complex nature of "acting-out." Suffice it to say that it represents behavior outside of the therapy sessions that expresses neurotic conflicts of various kinds, including at times the transference neurosis. The therapist, in listening carefully to the patient, must be always alert for picking up clues that acting-out behavior is going on outside the therapy sessions. This behavior is sometimes quite gross but at other times very subtle; the therapist must attempt to inhibit it and get the patient to convert it into verbal communication of thoughts, feelings, and conflicts.

Since it is a substitute for verbal communication and insight, it follows that gross acting-out behavior makes progress in psychotherapy impossible. It must be halted as a precondition for therapy or no therapy can take place. At times it is necessary to confront a patient with this fact in the form of an ultimatum. The therapist who ignores or makes no attempt to stop gross acting-out behavior is in a sense a partner to it.

Similarly acting-in is expressed by the patient's (or therapist's) behavior during the sessions. This can range also from gross behavior to subtle manifestations: sometimes it is very difficult to distinguish between acting-in and ordinary motor manifestations of the patient's personality.

Moreover, the therapist must watch in himself the temptations for acting-out and acting-in. The latter often appears disguised as various helpful gestures, but can also appear through the lack of an appropriate response. Most of us would respond rather quickly with communication to the attractive female patient who pulls her skirt up and puts her legs apart in the midst of a therapy session; but a lack of communication response to the same individual who sits in just such a way as to reveal a suggestive but not gross portion of herself is a form of acting-in on the part of the therapist. It is especially easy for therapists to rationalize acting-in of their own, just as it is easy for patients to amass arguments against the interpretation that they are acting-in.

The danger of acting-in and acting-out is that they represent the discharge and partial gratification of unmet needs, with a consequent lessening of communication and discussion of these needs. This works against "mutuality" and pulls the working alliance apart. Since the alliance is based on mutual observation and communication, such basic defenses against mutual observation and communication make the alliance untenable.

Thus, in a simple example, it is much better for the patient to come into his session and berate the therapist, after a while cooling off and exploring with the therapist where this is coming from, than for the patient to omit going to his session. Conversely, it is much better for the therapist to have it out with a berating patient than to find an excuse for missing or coming late to a session with a patient he anticipates will berate him.

The required conditions for an optimal working alliance to form and be maintained, therefore, are the inhibition of acting-out and acting-in on the part of both therapist and patient, a therapeutic atmosphere, an ego in the patient capable of certain key functions, and continual scrutiny through a mutual exploration of the state of the alliance.

Countertransference –We distinguish the term "counter-transference structure," borrowed from Tower (1956) from the terms "countertransference" (Reich 1951) and "countertransference neurosis" (Racker 1953). Although there is very little consensus in the literature on these matters, it is useful to make these distinctions especially when discussing healing factors in psychotherapy.

"Countertransference" represents fleeting manifestations in the psychotherapist of behavior, feeling, and fantasy in response to the transference *and* personality of the patient at a given time in therapy.

The "countertransference structure" is a consistent and relatively permanent aggregate of feelings, fantasies, and ways of reacting that develop in the therapist as a response to the transference and the personality of the patient over a long period of psychotherapy.

A "countertransference neurosis" is said to occur when the patient becomes more important to the therapist than anyone else in his life. Except possibly in certain situations involving the treatment of schizophrenics (Searles 1965) the countertransference neurosis is always pathological.

Although the subject of countertransference has been taken up by a variety of writers, it remains poorly delineated and subject to a confusing array of terminology. An example of this is in the well-known paper by Gitelson (1952) on the subject. He points out that Freud's original idea of countertransference was limited to meaning the reaction to the transference of the patient. He suggests speaking of "therapist transference" as a reaction to the patient as a whole and "therapist countertransference" as a reaction to partial aspects of the patient, whatever these aspects may be.

Orr (1954) points out other uses of the term "countertransference" in his excellent review of the subject. These range from countertransference being defined more strictly as a transference to the patient for whatever reasons, on the one hand, to countertransference defined as including everything that the therapist feels toward the patient, on the other hand. It is clear therefore that we are dealing with a variety of phenomena subsumed at times under one term; at other times the same term is used to denote only certain of the phenomena.

It seems impossible to separate except in a highly abstract manner the three crucial aspects of what is called "countertransference." These essential elements are:

1. Fantasies, feelings, thoughts, and behavior—"reaction"—to the transference manifestations and the transference neurosis of the patient.
2. A transference to the patient. In all close human reactions some transference is bound to take place. The nature of the transference, besides being based on the personality of the therapist, depends on various characteristics of the patient, both physical and psychological, regardless of whether these are presented as part of the patient's transference or his general personality.
3. A reaction, as defined above, to the various personality features of the patient.

These elements are all quite complicated and intermingled, and attempts to separate them result in artificial and arbitrary formulations.

Countertransference becomes an interference in therapy because it produces anxiety (Cohen 1952). Manifestations of this anxiety appear directly or indirectly through certain fantasies, feelings, and behavior in the therapy. The common usage of countertransference in recent texts on psychotherapy emphasizes element (2) in the definition of essential elements; that is, an irrational transference reaction from the therapist to patient. One would expect that this would almost invariably be an interfering factor in psychotherapy.

However, the matter is not as obvious as it seems. For example, when one uses a broader definition including all three elements, the examination of one's countertransference can reveal valuable information about the patient. Countertransference thus is an important tool for understanding the patient. A self-scrutiny, for it often can lead the therapist to new insights into those aspects of the personality of the patient that he otherwise finds himself responding to almost automatically (Wiegert 1954). It is a difficult form of self-scrutiny because these responses usually do not fit the therapist's ideal of how he should be and to study them requires the capacity to be objective about one's self.

Searles (1965) at times even discusses with the patient himself those aspects of the countertransference provoked by the patient's behavior and personality. This can be quite a valuable technique if used properly.

For example, a young divorcee was referred to me who had been to four psychiatrists previously for periods of four months to a year with no helpful results. In the first few sessions she was very dramatic and pleading for help with crying and longing for love. I began the treatment with focus on what she expected from psychiatry and psychiatrists and she became rapidly more rational and calm. However, after a time I noticed that I dreaded the sessions with this patient and felt exhausted after they were over. This was not simply a result of her focusing such cravings on me, as I had other patients like this in my practice and did not react with such irritation. It was so strong I seriously considered sending the patient to yet another psychiatrist, but since she had been to so many I decided as a last resort to discuss the matter frankly with her.

The discussion led to the uncovering of a pattern of interpersonal relations, beginning in childhood. She would present strong rescue wishes to various father figures, but when they reached out to her in response to the intensity of her longing, she would manage to push them away. With her husband, for example, she was "swept off my feet" by his strength and attention; after marriage she suffered from severe vaginal spasm and he could not penetrate with the penis. With me, as I sincerely attempted to understand something she said and would comment on it, she would leap on some word or phrase, distort it out of context, and feel either ragingly insulted or hopelessly despondent, depending on the distortion. She was really quite an expert at it, and had thoroughly exasperated the previous therapists. Careful and pointed discussion of this did not eliminate this pattern but muted it sufficiently so it was possible to work successfully with the patient.

In this example countertransference appeared as an interfering factor but could be usefully employed to uncover some extremely important material.

The solution to the countertransference problem cannot simply be more and more analysis. The indication for further personal therapy arises when either there is acting out of the countertransference or there is not sufficient awareness of the countertransference. There is *always* going to be countertransference. As Heimann (1950) puts it:

> The aim of the analyst's own analysis . . . is not to turn him into a mechanical brain which can produce interpretations on the basis of a purely intellectual procedure, but to enable him to *sustain* the feelings which are stirred in him, as opposed to discharging them (as does the patient), in order to *subordinate* them to the analytic task. . . .

Borrowing from Menninger (1958), the common ways in which countertransference makes its appearance "may be worth listing for their didactic value." These are:

1. Inability to understand certain kinds of material that touch on the therapist's personal problems.
2. Depressed or uneasy feelings during or after sessions with certain patients.
3. "Carelessness in regard to arrangements—forgetting the patient's appointment, being late for it, letting the patient's hours run overtime for no special reason."
4. Persistent drowsiness of the therapist during the session.
5. Over- or underassiduousness in financial arrangements with the patient.
6. Repeatedly experiencing erotic or affectionate feelings toward a patient.
7. Permitting or encouraging acting-out or acting-in.

8. Trying to impress the patient or colleagues with the importance of the patient.

9. Cultivating the patient's dependency, praise, or affection.

10. Sadistic or unnecessary sharpness toward the patient in speech or behavior, or the reverse.

11. Feeling the patient must get well for the sake of the therapist's reputation and prestige.

12. Being too afraid of losing the patient.

13. Arguing with the patient, or becoming too disturbed by the patient's reproaches or arguments.

14. Finding oneself unable to gauge the point of optimum anxiety level for smooth operation of the therapeutic process, as discussed previously.

15. Trying to help the patient in matters outside the sessions, such as in making financial arrangements or housing.

16. A compulsive tendency to "hammer away" at certain points.

17. Recurrent impulses to ask favors of the patient.

18. Sudden increase or decrease of interest in a certain case.

19. Dreaming about the patient.

20. Preoccupation with the patient or his problems during leisure time.

It is necessary to add a careful statement here to avoid misinterpretation. Those elements of countertransference that represent the unconscious transference from the therapist to the patient can often be interfering and it is usually unwise to encourage, act out, or discuss these elements with the patient. Those elements of the countertransference that are based on real provocation from the patient, however, are sometimes useful to discuss.

This leads to a most difficult and controversial question. Is the element of countertransference represented by an unconscious transference from therapist to patient ever desirable? The more orthodox opinion on this matter seems to be in the negative; in fact the persistent existence of this in the therapist is sometimes seen as indication for further treatment for the therapist. However, another point of view is possible, bringing into the spotlight such controversial terms as "corrective emotional experience" (Alexander and French 1946, Alexander 1956), "countertransference structure" (Tower 1956), and "core stage" of "symbolic synchronization and complementary articulation" (Whitaker and Malone 1953). This brings us to a discussion of after-education, the subject of the next chapter.

9

After-Education

The concept of after-education discussed by Freud (1938) "to correct the blunders of the parents," is controversial and has already been mentioned under previous headings. However, it is so important and so controversial that it deserves a separate focus.

First, one must carefully distinguish between *conscious* and *unconscious* after-education that takes place in psychotherapy. In conscious after-education there is a deliberate attempt either through intellectual instruction, role-playing, or attempts to provide "corrective" emotional experiences, to modify superego attitudes, or to improve ego function. This may be as simple as providing information for the patient. It may be as complex as Ferenczi (1926) and later Alexander and French (1946) proposed in their attempts to shorten the therapeutic process by deliberate behavior of the therapist designed to have a corrective impact on the patient. This impact is based on the importance of the patient experiencing as clearly as possible the difference between the therapist and the parent. It is generally accepted by now that authoritative approaches, information-giving, and deliberate role-playing, while of value at times in supportive psychotherapy, have only a very limited effect as healing agents.

Alexander (1956) is most emphatic that *the* crucial factor in psychotherapy is the experience by the patient of the difference in the reaction of the therapist from the reaction of the parents. Thus he writes:

> The course of the treatment consists in a long series of corrective emotional experiences, which follow one another as the transference situation changes its emotional content and different repressed childhood situations are revived and reexperienced in the relationship to the therapist.

The experiencing of the difference between the reactions of the parents and reactions of the therapist are more important than interpretations and these experiences constitute "the fundamental therapeutic factor," according to Alexander.

Saul (1958) writes more modestly. He asks, "What is the process which corrects the after-effects of the warping influences of the earliest years?" Saul sees the answer as a combination—details unspecified—of insight with the emotional experience of the transference, whereby the therapist replaces and corrects the superego, and "consequently corrects the id and ego." This comes about through "digestion of insights," working out of the sample human relationship to the therapist in the transference and testing what is learned in actual life.

Stone (1961) reduces the importance of emotional experiences in the transference much further. Although he feels that serious transference distortions will occur if the therapist does not feel a kindly and helpful, broadly tolerant, and friendly interest in his patients, it is unreasonable to expect the therapist to go beyond this. To maintain specific and consciously established attitudes permanently, whether loving or otherwise, which are not really a part of the therapist's identity, ". . . would impose a burden on the analyst, altogether incompatible with an honest and emotionally healthy life of his own."

It would appear that much of this argument could be resolved

by an appeal to common sense. Stone's phrase "physicianly vocation" is a common-sense type of approach to what we expect the
therapist to be like. We assume that the therapist has a healthy
identity of his own, with a reasonable superego and a relatively
mature ego, and therefore is capable of feeling kindly and helpful,
broadly tolerant, and friendly to his patients; to this we should add
"capable of being empathic with them," also. If the therapist lacks
these characteristics, regardless of under whatever theoretical pre-
text this lack is hidden, Stone is correct in predicting serious
transference distortions. If he possesses these characteristics, the
contrast with the warping parent will undoubtedly be most strik-
ing and be bound inevitably to have an effect of great importance
on the patient, whether we allow room for this in our theoretical
formulation or not.

Actual role-playing, on the other hand, carries the danger of
being at best phoney and at worst a countertransference acting
out, with which the patient is all too familiar from his past.

So much depends on the emotional and physical health, adequate rest, and adequate sources of personal gratification of the
therapist. It is hard to see how the common sense of this can
be refuted; the debatable point is the degree of emphasis to be
placed on the *relative curative importance* of insight and relationship.

Stone (1961) speaks of the experience of the physicianly vocation of the therapist as "normal" transference gratification. He
writes:

> In my view, if there is inadequate integrated transference
> gratification of this type, i.e., a failure of a palpable human
> relationship, incorporating an attitude intelligible and mean-
> ingful to the patient from the start, the technical transference
> and the transference neurosis are liable to have one or another
> spurious qualities; submissive-obedient, or frantically over-
> intense, for example.

Gitelson (1952) warns that trying to provide the patient with a "corrective emotional experience" can be countertransference acting-out, and a motherly or fatherly attitude felt as genuine toward the patient—with the obvious reconditioning consequences for the patient—can be attributed to unanalyzed character defenses in the therapist.

To complicate the matter further, Whitaker and Malone (1953) have focused an entire book on the *unconscious* aspects of after-education. This book has been considered controversial, and surprisingly little discussion of it has appeared in the literature.

Perhaps the best way to approach the concept of unconscious after-education is to begin with countertransference structure as conceptualized by Tower (1956). She attributes vital significance to an unconscious interaction between the transference of the patient and the countertransference structure of the therapist. She writes:

> The treatment situation between patient and analyst at its deepest and nonverbal levels probably follows the prototype of the mother-child symbiosis . . . and involves active libidinal exchanges between the two through unconscious nonverbal channels of communication.

To put it another way, Tower conceives of certain basic emotional attitudes toward the patient being generated into a consistent pattern of structure over the months and even years of working with the patient, and called the "countertransference structure." There is an interaction between the countertransference structure and the transference or transference neurosis of the patient, going on at various unconscious levels, that may be vital to the outcome of the treatment.

Menninger (1958) seems to imply a similar point of view, although, like Tower, he does not deeply explore this subject. His conception of a deeper and deeper regression taking place in psychoanalysis until a vital "turning point" occurs and the regression reverses with a "cure" as the result, immediately suggests the question as to *why* this reversal takes place. Menninger at first admits he does not know why, although at other points in the book he goes over the standard explanations of why cure takes place—without relating them in any specific manner to the way the "turning point" occurs. It is hard to know whether or not it was intended, but the implication of his conception of psychotherapy is that an unconscious emotional interaction is taking place between patient and therapist that leads somehow to the patient's gaining the strength to reach a vital "turning point."

At one point he speaks of the "*real* love" of the analyst for the patient as being a vital factor in producing the turning point. This is defined in terms of "physicianly vocation" but it makes one wonder whether more is not implied.

Hill (1955) suggests a mechanism of a more specific nature to explain the effect of the therapist's consistency and physicianly vocation. He asserts that the patient experiences this as "little bits of goodness," as discussed in detail in Chapter 5. The schizophrenic patient—and perhaps every patient—incorporates this into himself, and thereby experiences an increased feeling of goodness and self-esteem. Because this is an incorporation it is *not* experienced as coming from the therapist, and there is no praise for it. Although Hill does not mention it, this is exactly analogous to the enhanced sense of goodness, worthwhileness, and increased self-esteem that develops in a successful mother-child symbiosis by the same process. This is consistent with Tower's point of view quoted previously.

A much more extreme conception of psychotherapy was presented five years earlier by Whitaker and Malone (1953). According to these authors, through the use of certain techniques—including standard psychotherapy techniques—it is possible to "isolate" the therapist-patient relationship and hasten the transition in which this relationship becomes quite symbolic. The symbolic aspect of the patient-therapist relationship affords the opportunity for increasing regression until, at the "core stage" (see below), ". . . the patient achieves the gratification of certain infantile needs." This occurs through the relationship with the therapist and ". . . this gratification constitutes the effective force which shatters the neurotic process in the patient." Insight has little to do with it; for in the "core stage" the crucial healing experience is "primarily a nonverbal shared fantasy experience." Whitaker and Malone go to what must be called an extreme of recommending—cautiously—physical contact, including holding, rocking, and even spanking patients. In their view a symbolic transference gratification becomes the basis of a successful psychotherapy.

In this conception the unconscious interaction between patient and therapist is given *prime* importance. It is the duty of the therapist to effect a rapid transition as early as possible in the therapy from a real relationship to a symbolic relationship, which then moves through regressive stages until a "core stage" is reached. Both patient and therapist participate in a vital and affective way in this "core stage," which involves regression to "pre-transference" levels. At that point the therapist is "introjected" as a more satisfactory primordial parent. Infantile needs become more satisfied via this introjection, so the repetition compulsion is broken and the neurosis may be cured. It follows that the human or emotional participation of the therapist in a vital manner is what allows the patient to introject and utilize him as a more satisfactory parent imago.

Nacht (1962) has conceptualized this as the necessity of a certain "deep inner attitude" of the therapist toward the patient being fundamental for successful psychoanalysis. This deep inner attitude or participation is much more than the physicianly vocation of the therapist. It provides an atmosphere of peace and participation that of itself leads to growth via either introjection of a much better parent or direct gratification out of the therapeutic atmosphere itself. Thus Nacht (1963) speaks of the "gratifying presence" of the therapist, in which a silent and peaceful union can be established, satisfying an essential need in the patient. This is qualified by the warning not to allow the patient to attach "too firmly" to this kind of relationship, as eventually he must be brought to separation. Techniques for implementing Nacht's conceptions seem almost to require an intuitive capacity in the therapist, and are interesting but as yet vague and undefined.

Certainly the "atmosphere" of the therapist's office combined with his personality and inner attitude toward the patient provides a reconditioning or neutralizing effect upon previous destructive experiences from the patient's early childhood. This is especially true regarding deep anxiety produced by a highly ambivalent and intense relationship to one or both parents. This neutralizing effect by itself can be both gratifying and can liberate energy for growth, and so it can set the stage for introjection of the therapist as described by Nacht, Giovacchini (1965, 1967), and others. Surprisingly little work has been done in any effort to further conceptualize this mostly unconscious and extremely important interaction between patient and therapist. The so-called British School of psychoanalysts, including Klein, Fairbairn, Winnicott, and Guntrip (1968) have attempted to approach the problem using a highly controversial set of assumptions about infantile psychic processes. Although this work is interesting, it is very abstract and there is little that can be clinically confirmed—in fact, some of it presupposes operations taking place in the mind of the infant that are very complex indeed. Let us now reexamine the problem without over-burdening the discussion with assumptions about infantile ego processes more than is clinically necessary for understanding psychotherapy.

Most dynamic psychiatrists are willing to accept the idea that material presented by schizophrenic patients represents, in an extremely raw form, the same kind of psychic material that exists in us all, except it is more buried in us. Thus it is generally agreed that the study of schizophrenic patients—their behavior, thoughts, reactions, feelings, and fantasies—yields valuable information about the deep unconscious processes in all of us. One would expect logically, therefore, that investigations into the psychotherapy of schizophrenic patients would throw more light on deep unconscious interactions that go on in all therapy. It is a curious paradox, however, that generalization from the psychotherapy of schizophrenic patients to the psychotherapy of all patients meets with much greater resistance.

This paradox is understandable on psychodynamic principles.

In the psychotherapy of schizophrenics we deal with the most intense cannibalistic incorporation fantasies. Both the expression of these fantasies and the defenses against them are also extreme, and these hungry raging cannibalistic drives are focused quickly onto the therapist. Direct confrontation with such primitive and intense drives leads to defensive operations in the therapist to both protect him against the patient and also to protect him against his own primitive drives—which are invariably stirred up and resonate to the strivings of the patient.

Freud put his patients on the couch because he did not like to be stared at all day long. In "schizophrenese," this staring is often an hostile ocular incorporation process which quite commonly occurs. We are all familiar with the "schizophrenic stare." Imagine the great tendency of a therapist to resist being incorporated all day long by patients! One defense, besides putting patients on the couch or sitting beside, behind, or at all kinds of weird and unnatural angles to the patient, is to simply ignore the fact that at deep levels such processes are going on. Perhaps this is what most commonly happens, and those therapists who tend to concentrate on deep unconscious pregenital interactions are thought of as a bit extreme, or eccentric, or as the saying goes, "Up to his eyeballs in the id."

Searles, as we may all be thankful, is that kind of therapist. His *Collected Papers* (1965), especially the 1955 paper on *Dependency Processes in the Psychotherapy of Schizophrenia,* raises crucial questions about how to do psychotherapy, and warns of the danger from both the therapist's anxiety when bombarded by the dependency needs of the patient and the therapist's anxiety about his own infantile dependency needs, which are stirred up by the patient. Searles is against the direct material gratification of dependency needs of schizophrenic patients but does recognize, as discussed in Chapter 3, that the therapist gives a "gift" to the patient—". . . his consistent, attentive, receptive psychological presence with the patient during the therapeutic hour." Direct efforts to gratify dependency needs interfere with understanding and exploration of these needs. He is against a "compulsively loving" orientation to patients.

Searles in later papers does seem to agree with Whitaker and Malone that a nonverbal shared fantasy experience—a "core experience"—occurs in therapy. This takes place without "auxiliary techniques" or direct dependency gratification of the patient; it is in the nature of a symbiosis and, if therapy is to be successful, the symbiosis must eventually be resolved, according to Searles.

In the symbiosis, the patient is getting symbolic gratification of pregenital needs and the therapist is gratifying needs arising from the countertransference structure, as previously defined. The patient is basically introjecting a healthier parent object; Searles speaks of it as "a happy experience with a good mother" primitively expressed as a successful breast-feeding experience. After two months to two years* of this symbiosis, in which the therapist is also getting a contribution from the patient to his own personal integration, the patient's growth and resolution of the symbiosis are "innate." This is not difficult to conceive as analogous to the growth process in the child, where successful experiences in one stage release energy and motivation to move on to the next.

Searles conceives of the vital contribution from the patient to the therapist in terms of the need he claims to be present in any mothering one, for the child to help her with her personal integration, her maturing. As the patient realizes he is ministering to this need in the therapist, it raises the self-esteem of the patient. Thus, in the successful symbiosis the patient helps the therapist resolve further certain persisting "patient-vectors in the therapist," as Whitaker and Malone call it (see discussion below).

Searles believes that an important motivation that brings the therapist to work with schizophrenics is an unconscious seeking for help for that aspect of himself which is like a ". . . lonely, frightened, confused, hungry small child or infant." Therapists gravitate toward schizophrenic patients for this purpose because such patients have powerful strivings to "make contact with, and bring relief to, the similarly isolated frightened child in the parent."

Conversely the powerful striving to cure the parent or thera-

*This seems too short. Two years to four years in this phase is for me the more common clinical experience.

pist in schizophrenic patients tends to evoke, more than with neurotic patients, the therapist's need for therapeutic help. It is, of course, vital that the therapist be comfortable with all this, or he cannot be available or helpful to the patient. Searles therefore draws a clear although very controversial picture of the deep unconscious core interaction between the transference of the patient and the countertransference structure of the therapist in the treatment of the schizophrenic patients.

This conception seems to rest on the more general conception of Whitaker and Malone that in *all* psychotherapy both therapist and patient have both therapist and patient vectors in them."Therapist vectors" are responses to the needs of the immature child part of the other person. Most often the responses of the therapist are therapist vector responses to the patient; at times the patient responds with therapist vector responses to the relatively small residual immature child part of the therapist. "Patient vectors" are demands for a feeling response from the other person, much as a hungry child demands a response from his parents. It follows that the patient will get well only if the patient vectors of the therapist do not make excessive demands on the patient's therapist vectors.

Assuming that the therapist has had adquate therapy of his own, thus reducing his patient vector to a minimum, Whitaker and Malone then make the startling point that it is vital for successful therapy that the therapist bring his patient vectors along with his therapist vectors in a "total participation" with the patient. The therapist thus expands the frontiers of his own emotional growth via the therapy; if he refuses to participate totally in this fashion it is felt by the patient as a severe rejection and therapy is not successful.

It should be made clear that Whitaker and Malone draw a contrast between the "gross pathological patient vectors of the immature therapist" and the minimal or "sliver" type of residual patient vectors in the mature therapist. They insist, however, that every therapeutic relationship works on at least two levels; "the level of the apparent relationship and the level of the unconscious relationship." In the successful psychotherapy, a core symbolic process is passed through, resembling the mother-child symbiosis, in which the therapist gains further emotional integration and the patient introjects a much more satisfactory parent, thus breaking up the neurotic structure. This cannot happen unless the therapist is emotionally participating in the symbiosis with both his therapist vectors and his patient vectors.

The subject of this symbiotic fusion in psychotherapy has not received the attention it deserves. It has already been suggested that the reason for this could involve defenses in psychotherapists against their own cannibalistic and incorporation fantasies as well as against recognizing those of their patients. At the deepest intrapsychic levels in fantasy this fusion contains elements of a mutual introjection, which is certainly a most buried and primitive process.

The author has pointed out (Chessick 1966, 1968) the importance of a "locked-in symbiosis" between therapist and patient in the psychotherapy of borderline patients. In these patients it is seen as a vital prerequisite to the opening up of repressed narcissistic fantasies that form the center of the patients' lives, formed as a consolation for the disastrous reality of their childhood.

Giovacchini (personal communication) writes:

> I agree that the symbiotic fusion with the therapist is of crucial therapeutic importance for I feel it is through this fusion that the patient regains lost parts of himself.

Freud (1923) wrote that "the ego is a precipitate of abandoned object cathexes." Based on Freud's brilliant conceptualizations of the ego and the id, psychotherapy can be seen as directed primarily to the modification of ego functions and therefore, in a more basic sense, directed to the "abandoned object cathexes" (introjects) that make up the core of the ego.

Giovacchini (1965, 1967, 1967a) has devoted considerable attention to this kind of approach. He stresses the removal of "destructive introjects" in patients with character defects. He sees the

regressive sequence as it occurs in the formation of the transference neurosis, accompanied by correct interpretations by the therapist, as the primary way this is brought about. The introjects are
projected in the transference and dissolved by interpretation and
insight. A severe disorganized state may have to be passed through
during this process.

At this point Giovacchini (1965) differs radically from Whitaker and Malone. Although he agrees that a fusion with the therapist takes place, he characterizes it primarily as a fusion with the
"analytic attitude" of the therapist—that is, his nonanxious "investigative" (Searles) or "physicianly vocation" (Stone) attitude toward the anxiety of the patient and toward the destructive
introjects appearing in the patient. In patients with character defects, whom Giovacchini is primarily discussing, this attitude is
". . . an entirely new experience" and is introjected alongside of
the destructive introjects. This attitude, as well as "integrative
interpretations," are experienced as supplies coming from the
therapist analogous to what the adequate mother supplies in per-
ceiving and responding to her child's needs.

In fact, Giovacchini flatly disagrees with the whole concept
of Whitaker and Malone, opposing the gratification of the unconscious irrational demands on the therapist even in a symbolic way.
He insists that this contributes to the maintenance of the infantile
organization and equilibrium, one that contains a preponderance
of primary process elements.

> . . . whereas the therapeutically desired development and
> synthesis always heads in the direction of the secondary proc-
> ess. *The incorporation of an interaction that is based on primary
> process operations cannot become a basis for ego development.*
> (Italics added.)

Thus, the incorporation of the therapist is not a *gratification*
fundamental to successful therapy but rather provides an "attitude" in the patient alongside of disruptive introjects that makes

formal analysis of the transference neurosis possible. What is incorporated are certain attitudes and functions of the therapist, which provide an environment for the ego to expand its adaptive capacities.

It seems rather artificial to make this distinction. If introjection of the therapist takes place there must be an element of gratification in the transference that occurs. The crucial questions are whether (1) this element of gratification is *the* vital element in successful psychotherapy, as Whitaker and Malone argue; whether (2) it is of little importance one way or the other as compared to the analysis of the transference neurosis, as the classical Freudian would probably argue; or whether (3) it is actually detrimental to therapeutic process because it preserves the infantile organization, as Giovacchini contends.

It is not possible to resolve this vital difference of opinion by appealing to differentiations such as between diagnoses of patients being discussed or between therapeutic techniques used, for example, psychotherapy vs. psychoanalysis. For if these introjection processes take place, it either is or is not maintained that they are vital for success in any intensive treatment, and differing views are then expressed regarding what is fundamental to psychotherapy or psychoanalysis of patients with similar diagnoses.

It should be noted that in order to discuss this matter rationally, the therapist must be prepared to admit at least the possibility (1) that he gains in ego integration or emotional growth from the relationship with the patient, and (2) that he has patient vectors, that is, he unconsciously reaches out for a symbiotic fusion with the patient.

Let us turn now to personal clinical experience in the hope of understanding after-education better. Because I have been concerned with the question of how psychotherapy heals for a number of years, I have paid particular attention to these processes when I could observe them in myself and in residents I was supervising. The answers were somewhat disappointing in that no consistent trend emerged that could be clearly correlated with success or failure of treatment.

My experiences from long-term intensive psychotherapy of

patients and supervision of residents who were attempting to do the same are listed as follows:

1. Schizophrenic patients tend to bring out the pathology of the therapist. This seems not so much a function of their desire to heal or hold together the mothering one as it is due to the direct focus on the therapist of extremely primitive fantasies, in an intense and often poorly controlled way. The therapist finds himself defending against being the object of such primitive fantasies and against his own primitive fantasies, which are stirred up by all this.

2. Adolescent patients have a special capacity for growth by introjection of attitudes and ego functions of the therapist, in the sense that Giovacchini is talking about. Some authors would argue that this is "identification" (Schafer 1968). At the same time such growth is not into as stable a structure as we should like—there is even a tendency of adolescents to put the therapist on and off like a mask, depending on the circumstances. Because of the nature of therapy with adolescents, I think we see the purest case here of minimum symbolic unconscious gratification from the identification or introjection of the adaptive capacities or attitudes of the therapist, and maximum benefit from the operation of the newly incorporated attitudes and ego functions themselves.

3. The only reasonable approach to the vast majority of one's patients is that of a nonanxious, investigative, concerned human being, based on a "physicianly vocation," with all that implies. Any other "role-playing," compulsively loving, or auxiliary techniques eventually backfire unless one is interested only in immediate dramatic changes without concern for lasting improvement. Conversely, if one wishes to produce dramatic changes in people, *any* weird or overwhelming assault, whether it be bottle-feeding or electric shock, affords the best chances of producing such effects. This sometimes impresses the patient's family, but invariably backfires in the long run because it promises more omnipotence than the therapist can really deliver.

4. Any acting-in behavior, especially either punitive behavior, such as spanking patients or erotic behavior such as kissing, fondling, or allowing patients to sit on one's lap—no matter how well

rationalized—represents nothing but acting out of countertransference problems of the therapist and presents the double harm of not only stalemating psychotherapy but destroying trust in any future therapist.

5. If the reasonably mature therapist follows the above precepts, a certain therapeutic atmosphere will be present into which most of his adult patients will be introduced. A very complex interaction then takes place, involving both the needs and defenses of the therapist. The following outcomes may take place:

Patient and therapist emotionally engage on a mostly symbolic unconscious level, in a process that affords the patient sufficient gratification so he can correct a preverbal disaster, introject the therapist as a better parent imago, and grow.

Patient, for defensive reasons or for reasons in the personality of the therapist, keeps therapist emotionally at arms length and this symbiotic relationship does not take place. However, there is a working alliance, and the patient utilizes the therapist's attitudes and interpretations to improve the adaptive capacity of the ego. The patient refuses, however, to let the therapist into his emotional life directly. There is no correlation between diagnosis and choice of how the patient will use the therapist; it seems much more correlated with the personality of the therapist and the life experiences of the patient.

For example, with a male therapist, a patient who suffered a destructive and cannibalistic mother but who has found in childhood that her father offered some peace and protection in the situation would more likely be willing to enter into a symbiosis. Another patient, who had a brutal paranoid father, would not. Even though she recognized the differences between therapist and father, the experiences with father were too disastrous to ever permit such a closeness with a father imago. Yet there was enough ego capacity to utilize the therapist indirectly and in so doing to grow.

The point is that patients will often make of the situation what they want in spite of our theoretical preconceptions, and at times they are correct in their perception of what they need or what they can accept in order to grow. The therapist has to offer the proper atmosphere and be sufficiently flexible to allow for various kinds of utilization of himself—without trying to force any patient into theoretical preconceptions.

Furthermore, whether or not a vital unconscious symbiosis will take place is a function of the particular personality of the therapist. With a different therapist the patient may utilize the therapy in a different way. Therefore, it is a mistake to speak of psychotherapy as healing in only one way, and to insist that if that way is not followed—whether it be the interpretation of a full-blown transference neurosis or an unconscious symbiosis with the therapist—healing will not take place. This underestimates the flexibility of patients and their capacity to find what they need from a decent therapist regardless of his theoretical orientation—sometimes in spite of it. It also underestimates the complexity and variety of potentials for healing in the therapeutic relationship.

By viewing each patient as a challenge to the potentials for healing in the therapeutic relationship, one is constantly learning flexibility and the capacity to become a useful instrument for the patient. I believe this approach greatly maximizes the number and types of patients that can be healed and accounts for the poor predictability of all the theoretical orientations about which patients can be helped by psychotherapy and which cannot.

On the other hand, it becomes clear that no single theory of how psychotherapy heals can satisfactorily explain the process of cure in psychotherapy. It is evident that a number of processes take place simultaneously in each case, and those aspects of the therapeutic process that are of crucial importance in one case may be of little relevance in another.

In such a multiple-factor analysis of the therapy process, the best we can do is isolate out important aspects of the process such as working through, after-education, and the like, and make sure that the training to become a psychotherapist involves close attention to the understanding and mastery of all of these factors.

The therapist will have to judge, studying each of his patients individually, which aspects of the therapy process have the greatest relevance for that patient. This requires a far greater maturity and flexibility from the therapist than the more orthodox conception of the therapist as an adherent of one school or another, trying to apply the same conceptions—and sometimes rather stereotyped and dogmatic preconceptions—to every case. Maximum flexibility and understanding of the therapeutic process by the psychotherapist will thus guarantee the highest possible percentage of successful cases.

10

Conduct of the Psychotherapist

Montaigne wrote, "The conduct of our lives is the true mirror of our doctrines." The modern psychotherapist, engaging in "conversations with therapeutic intent," as described by Schofield (1964), has an affinity to the ancient Socrates. In fact, there is a close parallel between the intellectual goals and methods of modern psychotherapy and the fundamental premises of ancient Greek philosophy. In addition, the modern psychotherapist has an opportunity, rare indeed in this age, to live a life approximating the "good life" as described by Hellenic tradition.

According to that tradition, there is an intimate relationship between knowledge and the good life. Therefore, if the therapist is not living a "good life" there is a serious inconsistency. For if the therapist does not have the knowledge to achieve the independence that comes from what the Greeks call "self-mastery"—*eukrateia*—then he disqualifies himself from being able to help others to realize their potential for finding the true freedom that develops with knowledge.

In today's terminology we would say the therapist has too many unresolved problems of his own, leading to excessive countertransference difficulties that result in what Searles (1965) has

called "the counter-transference-ridden flounderings of the neophyte."

Greek classic tradition, beginning with the philosopher Py-
thagoras, repeatedly emphasizes that *it is disinterested enquiry that
is the good*. The objective of "disinterested" pursuit of truth for its
own sake is seen as the best goal of life, and a life devoted to such
pursuit is the good life. Conversely, we have the famous maxim
of Socrates: "The unexamined life is not worth living."

Freud's conception of the unveiling of the unconscious as
making known what the patient already has known is obviously
related to the Socratic tradition of dialectical enquiry (see Chapter
16). The importance of this method in philosophy is illustrated by
Russell's (1945) remark that philosophy itself could be defined as
the sum total of those enquiries that can be pursued by such a
method. *This is the kind of thinking that does not permit a man to
close himself.* As Jaspers (1957) proclaims,

> It will not put up with the evasions of those who refuse to bare
> their innermost thought; it shakes the complacency of those
> who trust blindly to fortune, who content themselves with a
> life of the instincts, or who become too narrowly involved in
> the interests of personal existence.

Following the classic tradition it is easy to see that the correct
practice of psychotherapy is closely related to living a life devoted
to the disinterested pursuit of truth, with the tremendously important additional humanistic value of helping other human beings.
Thus it has a high value as a "good life" in the traditional sense,
if it is lived honestly, devotedly, and consistently.

Every therapist must undertake a continuous "disinterested"
lifelong striving for understanding himself. We hope this will lead
among other things to relative freedom from crippling of the
therapist by his own unresolved infantile problems. As Saul (1958)
points out:

The child lives in the analyst as in everyone else; only one expects the child to be a little less fractious, unruly and disruptive in those whose profession it is to help others in life's journey.

Only then can the therapist attain the state of unself-conscious alertness required for empathy with patients, and the ability to really listen to his patients.

The conduct of the psychotherapist, the kind of life he leads and the values he cannot help transmitting to his patient, are of vital importance in psychotherapy. These matters have not at all been sufficiently emphasized. Two of the most crucial factors in psychotherapy depend wholly upon the conduct of the psychotherapist. These are, first, the capacity of the therapist to empathize with his patients and, second, the development of trust on the part of the patient—trust in the therapist's integrity and basic warmth and humaneness. I will proceed to examine both of these crucial factors, depending so much on the conduct of the psychotherapist, in detail.

Fromm-Reichmann (1950) argues that:

We know now that the success or failure of psychoanalytic psychotherapy is . . . greatly dependent upon the question of whether or not there is an empathic quality between the psychiatrist and patient.

"Empathy" is not something that a person can put on or off. It is not primarily intellectual; it is not a role; instead, it is akin to what Nacht calls "a certain deep inner attitude" in the therapist that Nacht considers to be decisive in therapy (1962). Fenichel (1945) wrote:

... empathy consists of two acts: (a) an identification with the other person, and (b) an awareness of one's own feelings after the identification, and in this way an awareness of the object's feelings.

When we take the position of another person, our imagination projects out of ourselves and into the other person. We may experience certain changes in our own muscles and actual physical posture. To empathize does not mean that the individual must experience physical sensations; empathy can be physical, imaginative, or both. Even when it is "imaginative," it is more than "intellectual." With or without identifiable organic sensations, empathy still connotes a form of personal involvement and an evocation of feeling. Our empathy is no less real if our bodies undergo no physical change and if we move into the situation of the other person only in our fantasies.

This description, which is presented by Katz (1963), is enlarged by him as follows:

In face-to-face encounter we feel the contagion of attitudes and feelings of the other person. . . . Other response is triggered by cues in the conversation or by impressions we receive of the state of mind or feeling of the other person. We pick up signals through a kind of inner radar and certain changes in our own emotional state make themselves felt.

Perhaps no author emphasized the importance of empathy in his psychologic theories as much as Harry Stack Sullivan (1953). He never really defined the term but spoke of empathy developing through "induction" and referred to how the tension of anxiety present in the mothering one "induces" anxiety in the infant. The process by which this induction takes place he referred to as a manifestation of an interpersonal process that he called empathy. He wrote:

I have had a good deal of trouble at times with people of a certain type of educational history; since they cannot refer empathy to vision, hearing, or some other special sense receptor, and since they do not know whether it is transmitted by the ether waves or air waves or whatnot, they find it hard to accept the idea of empathy. . . . So although empathy may sound mysterious, remember that there is much that sounds mysterious in the universe, only you have gotten used to it; and perhaps you will get used to empathy.

Sullivan also introduced the term "empathic linkage," meaning a situation in which two people are linked in such a way that one is inducing a feeling in the other.

Fromm-Reichmann offered a dramatic example of the empathic process as she conceived of it (1950). She explained how "some empathic notion for which I cannot give any account" made her turn back toward a patient with consequences that later marked the beginning of successful therapy of that patient. This example, like Sullivan's definition, leaves empathy as a rather mysterious intuitive process and demonstrates empathy by the presence of a response in the therapist that can be observed by the patient or by an observer.

All seem to agree that the use of empathy in psychotherapy calls for a pendulumlike action, alternating between subjective involvement and objective detachment. It may be called a regression in the service of the ego when it is used toward specific goals. When the good empathizer regresses in the service of the ego, he engages in a playful kind of activity as he inwardly imitates the events in the life of his patient that may be current as well as past. His activity is regressive only in the sense that it calls for a relaxed and unstructured experience that we associate with the fantasy of the child or the poetic license we grant to the creative artist.

Empathy implies a certain investment in the patient on the part of the therapist, and the capacity of the therapist temporarily to fuse ego boundaries with the patient. At the same time this must be done in the service of the ego, that is, for a goal-directed purpose of feeling in the shoes of the patient. The therapist must then be able to swing back to an objective and detached relationship in order to make clinical use of the information gained through the empathic process.

Many authors have stressed the value of empathy in psychotherapy as a most important way to understand the patient. Kohut (1959) writes:

> We will take for granted, from here on, that introspection and empathy are essential constituents of psychoanalytic fact finding. . . . Perhaps we have neglected to examine the scientific use of introspection (and empathy), have failed to experiment with it or to refine it, because of our reluctance to acknowledge it wholeheartedly as our mode of observation. It seems that we are ashamed of it and do not want to mention it directly; and yet—with all its shortcomings—it has opened the way to great discoveries.

A careful discussion of "empathic thinking" and the use of it in dream interpretation is presented by French and Fromm (1964). These authors stress "empathic understanding" as a direct intuitive communication between the unconscious of the patient and the unconscious of the therapist. The patient evokes in the therapist "an empathic sense of what is going on" in the unconscious of the patient. Freud spoke of a "resonance" between the therapist's unconscious and that of the patient. This resonance enables the therapist to understand the language of the patient's unconscious. French and Fromm pointed out that there must then be a translation from this "empathic understanding" into a language suitable for scientific analysis. This translation is termed "conceptual analysis" by these authors. Thus we have again the pendulumlike action described above.

The therapist cannot pretend to have empathy for the patient if he does not happen to experience it. The pretense of empathy backfires because the patient can eventually discover his therapist's true feelings and lack of empathy. On the other hand, when the therapist's empathy is real, the patient will hopefully sooner or later recognize its genuineness. Similarly, if there is true empathic concern for the welfare of the patient, the therapist can be protected from being deluded by superficial progress. If he is able to empathize actively, he will not lose sight of objective danger signals that arise in therapy.

It is the anxiety of the individual therapist, so often disguised and unrecognized, that makes him the most prone to err. Anxiety pulls him back from intimacy with his patient for fear that something will endanger him. This is analogous to disruption of the mother-infant relationship as described by Schachtel (1949):

> The mother can be turned fully toward the infant only if she has an attitude of tender care. Anxiety and tension disrupt such an attitude; dislike is the opposite of it. This kind of "emotional absence" of a person is familiar to our adult experience just as we can be aware of the suppressed hostility of another person.

A great barrier to empathy is formed by unanalyzed narcissism in the therapist. In this situation there is a failure to be empathically aware of the patient and in this sense a failure in reality testing. The vision of the therapist is cut off so that he can experience only himself, his values, and his needs when in fact he should be apprehending and evaluating the world that belongs to the patient.

Unmet needs of the therapist may cause empathy to become the means of his achieving personal satisfaction. This is a form of self-indulgence and the boundaries of private need and professional responsibility get mixed, with the result that the patient is cheated of the insights he has a right to expect from his therapist. The pendulum fails to swing back to the objective because the empathic relationship is gratifying the therapist's unmet needs.

The more adequate the personal life of the therapist and the more vigilant his own sense of professional ethics, the less frequent and the less impulsive will be such moments of self-indulgent fantasy. The more secure the therapist and the more rooted in an identity of his own, the less he will be tempted to project himself into the patient's experiences as an envious imitator. The private world of the therapist must have a dignity of its own, offering personal gratifications and status gratifications. If he must use the therapeutic situation to make up for the poverty of his private life he will be taking from rather than giving to his patients.

A facet of this, often in my opinion not sufficiently emphasized, is the importance of adequate sleep, leisure, and vacation time and a reasonable freedom from various personal harassments and economic pressures. These conditions are mandatory if one is to have energy and inner freedom to empathize with patients.

Another danger is the tendency of the therapist to identify himself with the fixed routines and traditions of his profession. Empathy calls for flexibility and willingness to enter into new, unprotected, and unexplored areas. Each new patient has some unique quality that calls for a personal and unprecedented appreciation. The therapist errs if he relies on standardized techniques or uses only the diagnostic categories that his predecessors and colleagues have defined for him. He must venture alone, personally and privately, into the inner experience of another person. Even when he has become familiar with this individual, he cannot apply a label or a classification and feel complacent about his understanding.

The therapist can become so absorbed in professional skills and techniques that his relationships with patients become depersonalized. Often the gestures of empathic communication are made, but the reality and the freshness of the meeting are lost and in their place an almost inevitable artificiality intrudes. When this occurs, it reflects a lack of vigilance on the part of the therapist; he loses part of his own humanity and slips into the habits of the bureaucrat, for routine is comfortable and apparently efficient.

I have recently discussed "vanity" and "greed" as important factors interfering with empathy (Chessick 1967a). Although these are somewhat superficial and rather philosophical terms, one is continually impressed with the pressures in our culture that seem superficially to promote vanity and greed and even to reward it. As Freud (1930) wrote:

> The impression forces itself upon one that men measure by false standards, that everyone seeks power, success, and riches for himself and admires others who attain them, while under-valuing the truly precious things in life.

Greed can be understood as being derived from a variety of unresolved childhood conflicts, leading to overemphasis on acquisitiveness. This usually appears as an excessive preoccupation with the accumulation of money and the various substitutes for it such as cars, boats, diamonds, and the like. On a more subtle level there is a preoccupation with having acquisitive needs met in the psychotherapy, either vicariously or even directly. Anyone engaged in the supervision of neophytes in psychotherapy sees the amazing variety of ways the patient and psychotherapist arrange to satisfy the needs of the psychotherapist. Finally, greed can lead to a preoccupation with power. Attaining a high rank or status in the academic or professional world or in the community gratifies greed in an indirect fashion by the reassurance that one's needs will be given first consideration over that of one's neighbors or colleagues.

Vanity connotes the adolescent derivatives of greed, such as the excessive need to be praised, admired, envied, or highly respected. There is preoccupation with being a "big man," "noted," "influential," and an "authority" in the field. The most unfortunate aspect of vanity is its tendency to feed upon itself. The more praise and envy, the greater the vanity and the wish for more. On a deeper level, early narcissistic wounds in the therapist must be constantly salved.

When greed and vanity are strong, the patient receives a

double message from the therapist. On the one hand there is a lip service to the classical ideal of the disinterested pursuit of under-standing the patient—unless things have progressed so far that the "authority" is preoccupied with presenting the patient with his "new" method. On the other hand the life patterns of the therapist demonstrate an entirely different set of values. It is amazing how quickly even the sickest patient catches on to the life patterns of the therapist, regardless of efforts to maintain "neutrality" or "anonymity." Perhaps thinking that one's patients cannot catch on to one's personality patterns is an extreme form of vanity!

The sicker the patient, the more destructive to his therapy is this double message. Healthier patients can confront the therapist and often choose to leave treatment and find a healthier therapist, but severely disturbed patients are too overwhelmed by their de-pendent needs to leave the "authority," whose office atmosphere and personal demeanor promise the omnipotence to meet these needs. Such a situation guarantees stalemate, at best.

If vanity and greed cannot be overcome by application of inner dialectic it is an indication for return to further personal psychotherapy for the therapist. Another alternative would be to leave the field of psychotherapy and to devote one's self to the many other aspects of psychiatry, in which one's own problems cannot be such interference.

The loss of the therapist's empathic capacity and his humanity becomes an exceedingly important issue, especially in the treat-ment of borderline patients, but it can be absolutely destructive in any psychotherapy. Grinker *et al.* (1968) describe the Postgradu-ate Psychoanalytic Seminar at the Chicago Psychoanalytic Insti-tute, in which sixteen psychoanalysts met monthly to discuss their pooled borderline cases in various forms of treatment. Dr. Stan-ford Gamm, one of the seminar leaders, states (personal communi-cation):

> Even in so-called classical psychoanalysis one only deals with derivations of infantile conflicts. The nuclear conflict in the borderline patient is in the early very traumatic mother-child

relationship. The patient relives it in the transference and needs desperately to have a corrective *experience* with the doctor. Until the patient can trust the doctor sufficiently he can't relive the rage engendered by the mother, and the doctor's *"actual" behavior* determines *that trust* more than probably anything else. Here's where doctor's personality comes in.

A good example of this arises from consideration of the problem of payment for therapy (Chessick 1967c), a topic surprisingly neglected in the literature. The personal integrity of the psychotherapist is of paramount value to his patients and a significant expression of this integrity is the therapist's approach to a responsible financial relationship with his patients.

Schofield (1964) claims:

> The most promising procedure which thus far has been uncovered for management, treatment, and prophylaxis of the so-called functional mental and nervous sicknesses is a conversation which has therapeutic intent and occurs in a relationship of friendship. . . . These "advertising outcomes" of public education have created consumer demand, at all levels of the "therapeutic conversation" market, that far exceeds available resources.

These sentences can be read in two ways. If one wishes to give the author the benefit of the doubt, one can accept the idea that a certain spirit of "friendliness" is beneficial to unhappy people, and that "therapeutic conversation"—whatever that is—is worth paying money for.

At a more ominous level, there is the implication that psychotherapists are, in a sense, prostitutes, that is, they sell "friendship" —whatever that is—to people with "so-called functional mental and nervous sicknesses." A further step, but logically implied in this view, is that the therapist preys on the lonely and the unhappy.

For money he will tolerate the obnoxious person and guarantee the lonely person someone to talk to, saving them the trouble of acquiring the social graces necessary to make and keep friends.

On occasion psychotherapists surprisingly speak this way of themselves, usually in a melancholy or humorous manner. Actually, it is all nonsense. The mature psychotherapist does not sell friendship for the simple reason that friendship cannot be bought or sold, as the most elementary thinking about the meaning of the term will reveal. He sells his time and the professional skill acquired by virtue of his training and ability. If he tries to sell anything other than this professional skill he is, in my opinion, engaging in narcissistic countertransference acting out. This may lead to temporary improvement in the patient but certainly not to any lasting change. The most serious chaos takes place when the therapist attempts to heal the patient by tender loving care or by seduction.

There are, of course, numerous patients who are so damaged that they are unable to engage in psychotherapy as an explorative process. A few patients in my practice are even so disturbed that I am the only human being to whom they ever talk in a personal manner. It appears that the relationship with me is all that stands between their functioning in society versus their being in a mental hospital. Even such patients are not paying for "friendship"; they are paying for an effort that offers them *hope.*

A paranoid schizophrenic schoolteacher has been seeing me once a week for seven years. She has her psychotic ups and downs, but is enabled to function on the premise that she (legitimately) is in treatment and hopes to get well some day. Hope is of such a nature that it does not fade with time in some situations. Witness the Jewish people still waiting for the Messiah to appear, a hope that has kept them alive through the ages in spite of much persecution. In therapy, the patient's hope is predicated on the possession of professional skill by the psychotherapist, compounded in this instance by a charisma attributed to the therapist out of the desperation of the patient. Such a treatment has the same justification as the treatment of a patient with a serious malignancy. The physician does his best, the patient hopes for the best and attributes a certain charisma to the physician despite the grave reality of the situation.

If the psychotherapist feels that the primary product he has to sell is "friendship," this may be due to his misunderstanding the meaning of the word; he may even have a wrong conception of what psychotherapy is all about. This should not be confused with "therapeutic alliance" or with the "physicianly vocation" of the therapist (Stone 1961), both of which are vital factors in psychotherapy but certainly cannot be bought or sold. In the former, a gradual alliance is seen to develop between the observing part of the ego of the patient and the ego of the therapist for the purpose of examining and understanding the patient in spite of the pain and anxiety involved. In the latter, it is expected that a certain attitude, termed "physicianly vocation" by Stone, must be brought to any therapy regardless of fee, if the treatment is to succeed at all. Stone adds:

> . . . it is *not* an excessive expectation that an analyst, in his capacity as physician, feel a kindly and helpful, broadly tolerant and friendly interest in his patients. . . .

It is obvious that such feeling would have to be genuine and therefore could not be bought or sold.

Patients should not be manipulated. Therefore, except in certain very special situations in which the psychotherapist is convinced that the dynamics call for it, the fee should not be set with either the idea of doing the patient a favor such as professional courtesy, or of accelerating the therapy by setting an arbitrarily high fee. Freud (1913) already had some very common-sense attitudes toward the fee.

Alexander reported a famous case from his beginner days in which a more expensive therapist was more successful with a patient. Yet it is not necessary to draw the conclusion from this that the higher fee *per se* was the factor making the difference.

Why not the greater experience, skill, and self-confidence of the older therapist?

There are many cases of successful psychotherapy carried out by residents at no fee, or in public clinics at fees set by ability to pay. The fee should be set at the general going rate in the community, like that of any other medical specialist, and left there. For the majority of patients this is satisfactory; they come to their sessions and pay regularly. The subject becomes irrelevant.

In beginning a new therapy effort, it must be realistically determined whether the patient can actually afford to pay whatever the going rate in the community might be. This must be discussed frankly with patients, and there should be no hesitation to review budgets and to question faulty financial thinking.

It is unwise to set a higher fee for wealthy patients because this leads to countertransference difficulties, not only with the wealthy patient but also with the less well-to-do patient who may be competing for empathy and resonance in the therapist's unconscious.

The therapist who sets a ridiculously low fee or an unfairly high fee is engaging in countertransference acting out, regardless of the rationalization he uses. This includes the excuse that the case is "interesting," or "rare," or "worthy of publication." Nobody is likely to succeed in justifying a low fee during the years of bombardment by the full intensity of the patient's emotions, regardless of how "interesting" the "case" happens to be.

Occasionally patients act out in therapy and foolishly throw away a significant portion of their money, making further payment of fees impossible. Usually one can see this coming and head it off, but occasionally it is done so cleverly that one cannot. In such cases I discontinue treatment. On the other hand, genuine financial reverses do occur and in these instances I permit the patient to owe the fee, regardless of the amount, until such time as they can pay me. Under ordinary circumstances I do not permit debt to accumulate beyond one month; this means a treatment may be discontinued if there is no payment for two months.

It follows from the previous discussion that a psychotherapist in private practice should not begin treatment with a patient who cannot afford to pay the customary fee. This rule applies only to cases that are obviously going to be long-term—over a year or more in duration. In those exceptions in which one does not insist on regular current payment, it is after the first year that counter-transference problems begin to really pile up, especially when other patients are waiting to begin treatment.

In some cases it is possible to plan that the patient will be able to begin work after a year or so, and pay the customary fee. I have treated a number of patients successfully who had their first year sponsored at a reduced rate by the State of Illinois Division of Vocational Rehabilitation. In such cases the treatment was aimed at enabling the patient to be able to work; these were almost always borderline schizophrenics who responded sufficiently to supportive treatment to make it worth their while to go to work to pay for it.

Inflation is another consideration for psychotherapists. Over a period of three or four years the therapist may find it necessary to raise his fees. New patients are charged the new higher fee, of course, but what about old patients? It is cruel and unfeeling to make an across-the-board raise in fees of old patients. Each case must be individually discussed. Patients coming in more frequently than once a week may be unable to pay a raised fee unless a comparable increase in their income has occurred. Even some once-a-week patients cannot afford a raise in fee. For this reason some long-term patients will be still paying at a level charged several years ago. If the therapist is not greedy there should be no problem on this score; most competent psychotherapists are making comfortable incomes today.

There need be no great transference problems arising from fee raises if the patient and therapist discuss the matter frankly with each other, explaining personal needs and situations. Those patients who are looking for something to be angry about will be angry; this can be interpreted and dealt with in the relationship. Serious trouble over fees arises from impersonal handling, such as written notices, signs, sudden increases in bills without discussion, or informing patients through secretaries; these techniques indicate unresolved problems in the therapist.

In summary, we have discussed the importance of the conduct of the psychotherapist in this chapter, and described the many ways in which it can vitally influence psychotherapy. If the therapist does not live a "good life" in the classic sense of being devoted to the disinterested pursuit of truth, his countertransference problems will pile up. His conduct gives a clear message to the patient, regardless of what he may express verbally, and the presentation of conflicting messages leads to a "double-bind" situation obviously destructive to psychotherapy. Furthermore, his conduct and unresolved problems can lead to a serious interference with his capacity for empathy and can convert him from a humanist to a withdrawn and self-centered bureaucrat. The actual behavior of the therapist determines the trust that the patient desperately needs to have in him, and the handling of payment for psychotherapy is discussed as an example of how the conduct of the therapist is a mirror of his doctrines.

PART III

Special Contemporary Problems

11

The Vicissitudes of Anxiety During Psychotherapy

Anxiety has a crucial role in psychotherapy in many ways that have already been frequently pointed out. There is little agreement among schools of psychotherapy about the meaning and nature of anxiety, which justifies our concentrating on the subject. The theoretical aspects of anxiety from a "metapsychological" point of view are not of as much importance as the actual vicissitudes of anxiety as experienced by the patient in psychotherapy. The importance of the "titration" of the level of anxiety in psychotherapy has already been discussed in detail (see Chapter 5). One aspect of anxiety that is extremely fashionable these days and is becoming an increasingly common problem to psychotherapists is so-called "existential anxiety." A study of this problem will illustrate quite well the myriad problems with anxiety in psychotherapy.

In this chapter we will first attempt to arrive at a definition of "existential anxiety." Then we will discuss and illustrate manifestations of existential anxiety as they appear to the psychotherapist. The final section of the chapter will present a philosophical discussion of existential anxiety.

To serious thinkers the question "Is life worth living at all?"

has become central to our disappointing age. Numerous recent authors have claimed that this question is actually central to all thinking of all ages, and, indeed, that the "anguish" and limitation of human life play a vital role in determining all human thinking and behavior. Such claims bring the discussion out of the realm of pure philosophy and justify an investigation of the entire matter by psychotherapists.

Camus (1955) writes, "There is but one truly serious philosophical problem, and that is suicide. Judging whether life is or is not worth living amounts to answering the fundamental question of philosophy." This statement reflects the gradually increasing consensus among leading thinkers that life, rather than reflecting any "grand design" of God or gods, is an utterly meaningless and nonsensical phenomenon.

I shall take as a starting point and first postulate the observation of Kierkegaard (1946) that as scientific knowledge and technology increase, the inner sense of "certitude" in man—of knowing why he is alive and what for—decreases. The dogmas of religion have been challenged again and again by the advances of science, and at least the Western concept of "God" itself is under attack in our time from various points of view such as that of Freud (1927), who speaks of the entire matter as an "illusion" based simply on the wish for a powerful father to watch over us and take care of us. Religion according to this viewpoint becomes a matter of various magical procedures designed to influence the powerful Father.

The historical optimism at the turn of the twentieth century regarding the inevitable progress of man toward increasing reasonableness and happiness has been utterly devastated by two hot wars and a persistent "cold" war that have silenced human spirit everywhere and sown the widespread seeds of mutual hatred and perpetual distrust.

The religious wars of earlier days were replaced in this century by the "ism" wars, equally as ridiculous and hopeless in their goals. Even today men are grossly divided in the name of various "isms" and are utilizing scientific advance primarily for the discovery of more efficient methods of wiping each other out. There is little to even indicate that the species will survive all of this in the next hundred years or so, except what Santayana (1955) calls our "animal faith."

Unamuno (1954) points out that men philosophize in order to convince themselves, which they fail to do anyhow. He argues that philosophy is based on the longing not to die, a sequel of which is the desire for personal immortality. Unamuno describes this as an "inward affective problem"; he calls it the "tragic sense of life," that is, the realization that life is to end in death.

Reason and science are the obvious enemies of the affective longing not to die, for solution after solution that have convinced philosophers of their personal immortality have been devastated by scientific progress or by the development of new and better techniques of reason and logic.

The second postulate of this chapter agrees with Unamuno: In every man there is an inward affective yearning and longing never to die. Combining the two postulates, we can see that in every man there exists a longing not to die, in conflict with his rational knowledge of the meaninglessness and brevity of an individual's life. This conflict, which is basically insoluble, gives rise to an anxiety called by Tillich (1952) "existential anxiety."

Tillich distinguishes three main forms of existential anxiety, based on three directions in which "nonbeing threatens being." He labels these "the anxiety of death," "the anxiety of meaninglessness," and "the anxiety of condemnation." He regards pathological anxiety also as a form of existential anxiety "under special conditions." The main point is that the "fear of nonbeing" is at the basis of *all* anxiety, according to Tillich. The most outstanding example of "nonbeing," of course, is death or the extinction of our existence.

Existential anxiety is part of the human condition and is not anxiety that results from conflicts engendered in childhood. This latter anxiety, so familiar to psychotherapists, Tillich labels "pathological anxiety." Tillich's distinction between existential and pathological anxiety is unfortunately both inadequate and misleading, for it implies an importance to existential anxiety that must yet be demonstrated.

Great care is needed at this point so as not to become confused in a semantic problem. "Pathological anxiety," as used by Tillich, is analogous to "neurotic anxiety" as used by Freud. In his short book *Inhibitions, Symptoms and Anxiety,* Freud (1926) establishes the important conception of anxiety as a *signal* sent out by the ego to warn of an internal conflict between unacceptable impulses and repressing forces. It serves to mobilize the mechanisms of defense of the ego.

Freud takes quite a different view of anxiety, almost opposite to that of Tillich. Both authors agree on the general distinction between "realistic" anxiety—fear of a realistic danger to the organism from an external object—and "neurotic" or "pathological" anxiety. However, Freud (1926) regards the fear of death, when there is no immediate realistic threat, as an extreme form of the neurotic fear of the superego. The patient projects the superego onto the "powers of destiny" and fears abandonment by the protecting superego. His interpretation of the forms of "existential anxiety" of Tillich as described above would then be explained as:

> Putting it more generally, what the ego regards as the danger
> and responds to with an anxiety-signal is that the superego
> should be angry with it or punish it or cease to love it.

In *The Ego and the Id* (1923), written three years earlier, Freud flatly rejects the basic premise of Tillich:

> The high-sounding phrase, "every fear is ultimately the fear
> of death," has hardly any meaning, and at any rate cannot be
> justified.

He goes on to admit that a fear of death may be distinguished from "realistic" anxiety (fear) and from "neurotic" anxiety, and recognizes this as "a difficult problem to psycho-analysis." Working from his observations on melancholia, however, Freud believes that the fear of death in those individuals who are not being actually threatened with death from a realistic external source is a severe form of neurotic guilt arising through the mechanism described above.

The concept of existential anxiety has not received sufficient attention from clinical psychiatrists, although they must face it all the time both in themselves and in their patients. What is known about this entity from the point of view of the therapist in clinical practice?

In the first place we know that pathological anxiety may be *displaced* onto existential anxiety. Extreme anxiety and preoccupation with the boredom, anguish, nothingness, meaninglessness, and limitation of human life can be found in many pathological conditions such as depressions, obsessive compulsive neuroses, and borderline schizophrenic disorders, as well as in various free-floating anxiety states.

In these situations the anxiety from pathological problems is infused into the normal existential anxiety and supercharges it, or the depressive affect is blamed on the existential conflict. Thus the two kinds of anxiety and the "inner affectual problem" of Unamuno get all mixed up together and become hard to distinguish.

Psychotherapists tend to err in the direction of blaming existential anxiety too much on psychopathology; theologians and philosophers tend to err by exaggerating the importance of existential anxiety, especially when it is supercharged with pathological anxiety.

One may argue that existential anxiety in fact is a rather sophisticated phenomenon and requires a certain amount of ego strength to register at all. Although it is universal, there is little evidence to indicate that the masses of humanity are much influenced by it in their everyday behavior, in contrast to the all-pervading influence of the anxiety signal and pathological anxiety.

It is also possible to argue, as Marsh (personal communication) does, that the appeal of demagogues in politics, which is based in large part on the irrational fears of many people, could be an indication of the pervasiveness of existential anxiety. He adds:

> Also consider the tendency, described by Heidegger in *Being and Time*, of people to flee solitude, to lose themselves in the security of the crowd or "they," and to flee the anxiety which accompanies any genuinely personal exercise of thought or freedom.

Intellectuals and thinkers (who tend to be a bit on the obsessive and depressed side anyway) are prone to supercharge their ruminations on ontological problems with pathological anxiety and then to assume that everyone else feels these matters just as intensely. This is an error. Nietzsche (1969), very much in fashion with current existential philosophers, is a prime example of a severely mentally ill genius obsessed with an existential anxiety that reached the supercharged blinding intensity found only in schizophrenic anxiety.

A curious opposite twist to this situation, related to Rank's "birth-trauma" theory in which all anxiety is based on the prototype of the birth experience, is offered by Rheingold (1967). His thesis, the psychiatric analog of Tillich's emphasis on existential anxiety, is that a "catastrophic death complex" exists in us all, originating even in prenatal experience. Freud (1926) specifically rejected the idea of prenatal and birth experiences giving rise to a "basic" anxiety, pointing out that an ego was necessary before anxiety could be experienced.

At any rate, Rheingold argues that all women have secret "filicidal and mutilation impulses" toward their babies, which create a basic fear of catastrophic annihilation in everyone. He argues that existential anxiety, when experienced, is a defense against experiencing the true deep level of anxiety associated with the "catastrophic death complex."

It seems to escape Rheingold's notice that the theological debaters could turn his argument right around and contend that the catastrophic death complex is a defense against true deep existential anxiety!

Why do some people experience the existential anxiety much more severely than others, and what solutions are available for the treatment of existential anxiety?

The answer to the first part of this question seems to be a function of two factors. The first of these is the displacement described above, of pathological anxiety on to existential anxiety. People suffering from this are not hard to recognize clinically, as they manifest at the same time the other symptoms of depressive, obsessive-compulsive, anxiety, or borderline schizophrenic states.

The second factor relates to human differences in sensitivity and mental capacity. Why is one person enraptured by Bartok quartets and another bored to agitation? Why does one read Plato and another read *Playboy*? The majority of people are basically pleasure seeking and live from day to day; they just don't bother about these matters very much. They rely on established institutions to answer all their questions and they march off to the wars again and again—or is this their escape from existential anxiety?

However, it does not follow that all those who do directly concern themselves with these questions are neurotic or have an especially severe catastrophic death complex. Certainly some of them do. In psychotherapy we frequently see patients who seem preoccupied with the various aspects of existential anxiety. However, there is rarely a serious residue of "normal" existential anxiety left with such patients when the underlying neurotic determinants of this displacement have been worked through.

It is not always necessary, as Rheingold seems to suggest, that one must work through deeply repressed reactions to the mother's "filicidal and mutilational impulses" for this anxiety to disappear.

One might argue that existential anxiety disappears in psychotherapy because the patient unconsciously identifies with the unconscious defenses of the therapist against his own existential anxiety. Naturally, it is hard to find any evidence for this. Even if the therapist can become conscious of his own defenses against any true existential anxiety he may have, he does not usually see his patients imitating these defenses.

I now wish to present two clinical cases in which the patients seemed to be primarily preoccupied with existential anxiety. Such cases are not rare.

A. P. was a 29-year-old handsome man who began therapy in a state of almost psychotic collapse. Until 1962 he had been a brilliant and promising graduate student at a major midwestern university, working for his Ph.D. He was the favorite of the department and even took over the professor's course for him while the professor was away on a tour.

As the time for finishing his Ph.D. approached, A. P. began to become overwhelmed with the feeling that life made no sense, that it was all "absurd," everyone and everything was a fake, and all people were soon to die anyway. Suddenly one day in the middle of teaching a class he simply walked out of the classroom, packed his suitcase and left school. Not long afterward he got married and worked as a salesman.

During the marriage he had spells of silent withdrawal and depression during which he seemed essentially catatonic. He was unable to concentrate or do anything during these spells. At other times he would have fits of uncontrollable rage and would break the dishes and kick out the paneling on the door. Needless to say the marriage did not last and a divorce was obtained. In desperation he sought out psychotherapy, although he had little financial means. He was assigned to me for diagnostic work up through a community agency.

Even in the diagnostic interviews he displayed the same oscillation of moods as described above. In addition there was a flood of bizarre dreams and fantasies that plagued him, along with homosexual preoccupations. The history showed many attempts to escape the dreary boredom and "nothingness" that he felt, by traveling from city to city. At one point he wrote to me:

> I don't think you have any idea of the desperation I find myself in. Only to "split" (go somewhere else) is to give in to the ever present hope that somewhere life might be better. I don't know how much longer that might be the case, and

when I realize life is no better anywhere than here, then—I'm *begging* you to show me something to make it worth while.

I decided to give the patient a trial of psychotherapy both because of his brilliant past and because of his obvious reaching out, even though it took the form of his either insisting on prolonged intellectual discussions of the absurdity and meaninglessness of human existence or bursts of anger and outrage at practically anything I would say, sometimes even accompanied by threats of doing me physical harm.

Gradually I began to realize I was dealing with a basically gentle person, and as I became more comfortable with him it was possible to get some historical material and interpret his behavior in terms of his fear of his own dependency wishes and his attempts to get a "grip" on reality.

Mother was a fundamentalist who saw visions and made the patient go to revival meetings and kneel down up front to proclaim he also saw the visions and was "saved." The patient went through these rituals even as a child, knowing he was being a fake, and filled with the fear of sin and damnation. Father was a brutal policeman, who had no relationship with his son.

In therapy I did a great deal of listening and patiently allowed the patient to express his views about life over and over again. I dealt with these views on an intellectual basis, engaging in a kind of classroom discourse with him when he was calm enough to do so. At times the treatment resembled a seminar in philosophy or literature.

On the basis of this, the patient's intellectual interests began to revive and he resumed academic work and teaching. At no time over the first two years of psychotherapy was it possible to make *any* interpretation involving his problems with his parents that made any sense to him—he was so flooded with anger and guilt regarding them—and yet the therapy, based solely on our relationship, resulted in his successfully obtaining a Ph.D., a teaching position, and improvement in his relationships with people. I believe that his relationship with me gave him a structure and meaning to his life sufficient for restitutive forces in him to take over. The "existential" preoccupations dropped away by the end of the third year of treatment.

K. S. was a 20-year-old girl who appeared and acted about 14. She had been repeatedly hospitalized for schizophrenic episodes with overt paranoid fantasies of being poisoned and the like, and episodes of self-mutilation. Several psychiatrists had attempted to work with her but in the hospital she was extremely uncooperative and all sessions were spent either in dead silence or in battles about rules and regulations. Finally it was recommended she be sent permanently to a state hospital as a hopeless case. In desperation the family asked my help.

After a few sessions I felt that the patient was not dangerously suicidal or homicidal and that she was acting out some kind of bizarre drama in the hospital. She agreed to come in as an outpatient and so, to the horror of the hospital staff, she was discharged. She immediately began living in a different apartment every few days and sleeping with a succession of men and women. On a few occasions, when therapy stirred up anxiety or when I went on vacation, she would go to another city suddenly and without warning, but she would always come back.

After it became apparent that our relationship actually had some strength—most likely based on her wish not to be in a state hospital—I dared to explore what she was doing in greater and greater detail. In between spells of hallucinations, obsessive preoccupations, and various magical sensations, the patient reported a basic pattern of wanting to exist "outside of time." Her major deep concern was not to grow any older. Life seemed so meaningless and absurd that she didn't want to grow up until she found a way to give it meaning.

The only meaning to life she could understand at the time was in the fulfillment of secret narcissistic fantasies. She was the daughter of an extremely successful artist—who also felt that all life was absurd unless one could produce great creative work.

In order to solve this "existential" crisis, which had been growing worse each year of her life as she became older and older, the patient completely cut herself off from any kind of "structure" by which she could mark the days goings by. Thus the hospital greatly increased her panic. She could not stay in one place; certainly she could not work at anything or go to school. Unfortunately she did not have great creative talent so each successive year of her life made it apparent that she was not going to write the great novel or make the great scientific discovery. She was trapped.

In her life there were no object relations at all. Over the first three years of therapy I had to examine with her calmly again and again all sorts of episodes of behavior such as drug-taking, self-mutilation, and promiscuity until she gradually began to settle down in one place. It was possible to discuss her relationship with her parents in some detail, and this proved helpful at least on an intellectual level in that she began to accept the structure of psychotherapy and the approach of the psychotherapist and so form a solid therapeutic alliance.

Her problems gradually attenuated to the point where she could successfully hold a full-time job and the first "meaning" life began to have for her was (1) to become financially independent of her parents—a symbol of some beginning emotional independence—and (2) in the formal structure of her therapy appointments, which formed a consistent central routine in her life. The "existential anxiety" preoccupations did not disappear but they dampened down sufficiently for her to become a much more comfortable and functioning person.

In both of these extreme cases, one has a clear illustration of how severe existential anxiety can be a displacement from deep psychotic preoccupations involving the earliest ego-formative processes that were damaged by the pathological atmosphere of the mother-child symbiosis. This damage was at least attenuated by a relationship with the therapist and when the relationship "clicked" the preoccupation with existential problems tended to disappear.

The evidence from these and other cases indicates, in my clinical experience, that such existential anxiety is nonspecific, and can be present in a variety of types and kinds of problems. It is not necessary for a specific mother-child constellation to have

taken place, such as being exposed to maternal "filicidal and mutilational impulses."

In educated and intelligent patients existential anxiety can
form a difficult defense to deal with, somewhat on the level of
obsessive or paranoid symptoms, since such existential preoccupations always have more than a grain of truth in them. I find it best
neither to scoff at such preoccupations or to try to remove them
by "deep" interpretations, but rather to treat them as nonspecific
anxiety reactions that will drop away as the relationship with the
patient develops and deeper material can gradually be explored in
therapy.

It should be noticed that we are focusing so far on obsessive
preoccupation with "existential anxiety" as seen clinically to be a
displacement from pathological anxiety. Existential anxiety, when
freed from displaced pathological anxiety, is usually not a major
conscious preoccupation to people, although to some individuals,
because of an unusually sensitive makeup or philosophical bent in
their personality, preoccupation with it becomes a genuine problem.

When existential anxiety preoccupations appear clinically,
the psychotherapist finds he is often dealing with an individual
who is desperately trying to live up to a self-concept imposed on
him by someone else—deliberately or through early introjection
—rather than living up to his own identity. Such patients are
acutely aware of a feeling of the "meaninglessness" and "absurdity" of their lives, and when they can become free of the burden
of an externally imposed identity or set of goals these feelings drop
away. Christensen (personal communication) has been impressed
by the same phenomenon in his long clinical experience also.

To point out that existential questions become less overwhelming in the course of psychotherapy is not tautological if the
original preoccupation with existential anxiety represents a displacement from pathological anxiety. At the same time the extent
to which genuine existential anxiety drives and motivates human
behavior is most difficult to assess scientifically, and remains more
a philosophical than a tangible clinical question at present.

The remainder of this chapter will deal with the philosophical problems of "existential anxiety," to whatever extent such a phenomenon may remain when clearly detached from any displacement of pathological anxiety.

The theological and philosophical attention paid to existential anxiety lies in the philosophers' desires to convince themselves that life is worth living. Some use it as a springboard to "faith" or to the "God above God." If one is asked to take such an enormous jump over reason, a most powerful motivation must be supplied —hence the exaggerated importance of existential anxiety.

Unamuno (1954), for example, begs that when we have reached the "depth of the abyss"—when through the use of reason we have wiped away all hope of immortality and meaning to the world—we follow the longing and the passion and the will to believe in God. He writes:

> He who looks for reasons, strictly so-called scientific arguments, technically logical reflections, may refuse to follow me further.

He claims that faith, then, is the wish to believe, and to believe in God is justified by the wish to believe in God. Furthermore:

> In the same way, to believe in the immortality of the soul is to wish that the soul may be immortal, but to wish it with such force that this volition shall trample reason under foot and pass beyond it.

Thus Unamuno, in his mysterious way, is led from an inner affectual problem to a "pragmatic justification" for love, faith, God, and the immortality of the soul. There is simply no arguing with this point of view since volition "tramples reason underfoot."

Tillich's (1952) more careful discussion, which ends up rather disappointingly the same way, is worth reviewing because it reminds us of a virtue seldom discussed in the psychiatric literature: courage.

Beginning with Plato's *Laches*, it is clear that an exact definition of courage cannot be found. There is agreement that it represents more than bravery in battle. After reviewing numerous previous muddled definitions of courage, Tillich sidesteps the problem by speaking of a special kind of courage, "the courage to be." He writes:

> Nonbeing is omnipresent and produces anxiety even where an immediate threat of death is absent. . . . We try to transform the anxiety into fear and to meet courageously the objects in which the threat is embodied. We succeed partly but somehow we are aware of the fact that it is not these objects with which we struggle that produce the anxiety but the human situation as such. Out of this the question arises: Is there a courage to be, a courage to affirm oneself in spite of the threat against man's ontic self-affirmation?

Since Tillich doesn't ever really define courage, we must function with our intuitive idea of what it means. Nor is "nonbeing" really defined, but it is assumed to represent a mental and physical disintegrative process, accompanied by lack of realization of one's true potential and ending in death. If we agree with Tillich regarding the importance of this concept, then all human life can be seen as an attempt to avoid despair and the threat of nonbeing.

Furthermore, in Tillich's understanding of psychopathology even neurosis becomes a way of avoiding nonbeing, and so pathological anxiety becomes a form of existential anxiety. Here is the diametric opposite of Rheingold's hypothesis!

After this, Tillich becomes increasingly obscure. He seems to believe that neurosis represents a reduced self-affirmation in order to protect one's self from existential anxiety:

He who is not capable of a powerful self-affirmation in spite of the anxiety of nonbeing is forced into a weak, reduced self-affirmation.

Later on he requires a "balance" between "the warnings of fear" and "the courage to be" for a successful resistance to nonbeing. He does not tell how to achieve this balance.

At first Tillich seems to be essentially stating the Stoic position, which he calls "the only real alternative to Christianity in the Western world." Later he seems to be accepting the leap into Christian faith in stating that the courage to be always has a religious root. Again, this is so mysterious as to become impossible to debate.

What is one to make of all this? Are there no arguments against existential anxiety except to either totally relegate it to a manifestation of pathological anxiety or to exaggerate it in order to justify a wished-for religious structure?

Actually, there are two categories of solutions to the problem of existential anxiety. In the first category are a variety of fideistic resolutions such as advocated by Jung (1933) and many theological authors including those already quoted above. The intent here is not to quarrel with such solutions, only to point out that one is not driven by existential anxiety (assuming such anxiety exists and is a powerful driving force—an assumption not universally accepted) to *invariably* choose a fideistic solution. It is a matter of personal decision, and another category of solutions, which retain consistency with science and reason, is also available. I will conclude by reviewing this category of solutions; although the fideistic category has received much attention in the literature of theology, the other category has been almost completely neglected. Also, there is no reason why an individual could not choose to combine both categories of solutions! This represents the classical debate between Voltaire and Pascal; those who are intellectually curious lean towards Voltaire; while those who seek consolation choose Pascal (Torrey 1968).

The best antidote for existential anxiety is in the establishment of object-relations of a mature and truly loving nature. Love exchanged between husband and wife, parents and children, dear friends, and others, when truly related object love of a mature nature, greatly relieves whatever existential anxiety there may be.

One of the prime goals of psychotherapy is to develop the capacity to love in a mature give-and-take way, and this provides an additional reason why in successful psychotherapy existential anxiety tends to disappear as one learns more and more to give of one's self. (It is beside the point here to go into a lengthy discussion of "love"—the reader is referred to Fromm [1963]).

Many people have a damaged capacity for mature love that is not always amenable to psychotherapy, or for various reasons they have not received adequate treatment. The situation is not hopeless for them as two other defenses against existential anxiety are available, without involving mysterious abandonments of rational process and scientific argument.

First, there are the fine maxims and guidance of the Stoic philosophers (Oates 1940)—especially Epictetus and Marcus Aurelius, slave and emperor—which form a kind of primitive "courage to be." They do indeed offer an alternative to Christianity, are free from mystery, and contain exhortation to courage, with a keen sense of the hardness of reality.

The Stoic gospel is one of endurance rather than hope. This school took its name from where the founder Zeno (the Phoenician) taught, an open porch (in Greek, *stoa*). Their ideal of a single society, in which men act not for personal advantage but out of respect for the universal law, still has power to move us after 2000 years, as Jones (1952) reminds us. The Roman Stoics especially brought the earlier Stoic philosophy most in line with common sense. There is no substitute for reading the notes of Arrian, in which he presents the sincerity and simplicity of the doctrines of his master, Epictetus, and a similar extraordinary emotional experience awaits the reader on opening the "Meditations" of Marcus Aurelius.

The courage of Aurelius (and the other Stoics to a lesser extent because they carry the doctrine to the extreme of utter apathy and indifference), lies in his spirit of law and order, of balance and moderation, which we should accept. On the subject of death, for example, Aurelius writes:

> A man then that has reasoned the matter out should not take up towards death the attitude of indifference, eagerness, or scorn, but await it as one of the processes of Nature. . . .

His doctrine represents one of the most advanced attempts of man to conquer existential anxiety through the power of reason. The noted scholar Kaufmann (1960) refers to Freud as a Stoic "tempered by Freud's humor, his humility, and his humanity."

It must be granted that reason gives us only an intermittent and variable defense against existential anxiety but it can help to afford a satisfying defense for those who wish to base their lives on rational principles rather than blind hope.

A second temporary defense is afforded by the contemplation of beauty. If "thought" causes us to be aware of the meaninglessness and limitation of man's life, than we must be "teased" out of thought by the contemplation of beauty into a realm where pursuit is frozen and desire is stilled at least temporarily. Keats writes, in his "Ode on a Grecian Urn":

> Thou, silent form, dost tease us out of thought
> As does eternity: Cold Pastoral!
> When old age shall this generation waste,
>   Thou shalt remain, in the midst of other woe
> Than ours, a friend to man, to whom thou say'st,
>   "Beauty is truth, truth beauty,"—that is all
>   Ye know on earth, and all ye need to know.

Schopenhauer believed we could find temporary respite from the blind struggle of "will," which carries us relentlessly to our destruction, in esthetic contemplation. So, as a second defense, there is the possibility of immersion in the arts, which offers at least a backward extension of a man's life to communicate with the creators of the past, a communion with the universal human participation in beauty, and, for those lucky talented few, some creative contributions of their own.

Art alone endures, at least as long as man will endure and if one of his ridiculous political systems doesn't destroy or ban it all. Contemplating the beautiful is a transcending human experience that can be shared by all and is not mystical although it is difficult to describe.

In summary, the psychotherapist frequently has to deal with outbursts of "existential anxiety" in psychotherapy, which often represent a displacement from pathological anxiety. If the sources of the pathological anxiety are ameliorated either through insight or relationships, this "existential anxiety" tends to disappear.

To be preoccupied with whether or not life is worth living and the various manifestations of the absurdity of the human condition is, if it is not a displacement from pathological anxiety, a manifestation of existential anxiety. Genuine "existential anxiety" remains primarily as a philosophical problem, and it cannot be ascertained at present to what extent such concerns consciously or unconsciously generally motivate human behavior. There are no compelling arguments to elevate it to the status of neurotic anxiety as a motivating force in personality function.

It is not necessary to abandon reason in order to overcome existential anxiety or to make any mysterious "leaps" into religious faith; nor does the presence of existential anxiety offer any compelling reason to do so any more than the presence of any other form of anxiety. If one wishes to solve one's anxieties by mystical or fideistic procedures, this must be viewed as the adoption of a personal choice, not as an invariable principle of general human behavior.

Existential anxiety can be resolved either by the personal choice of fideistic solutions or by attempting to develop mature loving relationships with other people, or by both categories of solutions. Those who wish to avoid fideistic solutions can also make use of the Stoic philosophies and of participating in the communal human experiences of art and beauty.

It should be kept in mind that "existential anxiety" remains a controversial philosophical concept, and the importance of such "anxiety" as a general motivating force in human behavior has not been generally agreed upon.

12

The Borderline Patient

The best illustrations of the vital issues in psychotherapy discussed at length in this book come from a study of the borderline patient. In fact, this kind of patient puts every personal and intellectual resource of the therapist to a severe test. The ego of this patient will not tolerate the everyday pretenses and unspoken conflicting messages that mark the usual superficial or "social" contacts between people. He puts the therapist under a continuous glaring spotlight and is quick to pick up and to distort or exaggerate his unresolved difficulties and rigid adherence to bureaucratic routine.

Grinker *et al.* (1968) make a fundamental descriptive approach to the borderline patient. Their research is the easiest to describe, being characteristic of other publications by Grinker and his group. It consisted essentially of an attempt to delineate the "borderline syndrome" in a meticulous fashion. Patients generally diagnosed as borderline were observed, studied and rated, and a factor analysis was carried out on the data to discover general characteristics and subgroups. The overall characteristics found were (1) that anger was the main affect such patients experienced;

(2) that a defect in affectional relationships was present: "These are anaclitic, dependent or complementary, but rarely reciprocal"; (3) that indications of consistent self-identity were absent; and (4) that depression was based on loneliness rather than guilt. Four sub-groups were further delineated.

In their concluding material, the borderline syndrome is seen as based on "the basic defects in maturation and early development expressed in ego-dysfunctions." A variety of factors are believed to work on the development of this defect but the authors are not able to elucidate these factors.

The borderline patient has appeared with greater and greater frequency in literature of our day, just as he appears with greater and greater frequency in the office of psychiatrists. It is (1) the so-called borderline patient or (2) the depressed patient who reports in a clear fashion the feeling of being *unbearably alone.*

Litowitz and Newman (1967) have convincingly demonstrated how the "theater of the absurd" (Albee, Beckett, Ionesco, Genet, Gelber, and others) manifests the characteristics of the borderline personality ". . . just as the 'classical' theater (Sophocles, Shakespeare, Ibsen) parallels the content and conflicts of the classical neurosis." I believe that Brustein (1964) would agree with me in removing Ibsen from their list of the classical dramatists—Hedda Gabler, for example, would belong in the borderline category—but the basic thesis of Litowitz and Newman makes a lot of sense. The authors choose for special study two plays that are certainly among the best of the "theater of the absurd," Beckett's *Waiting for Godot* and Albee's *Zoo Story.*

Waiting for Godot is unforgettable as a demonstration of the deep loneliness and emptiness of the inner world of the borderline individual, as well as the dogged persistence, at the expense of any attempts to adjust to reality, of hope for miraculous rescue: "When Godot comes everything will be all right." The authors present a succinct review of the literature on the borderline personality and compare it with the material in the plays in a well-organized and convincing manner.

These patients are generally considered difficult and even undesirable from the point of view of the practicing psychiatrist.

Many of them previously received various forms of treatment with no noticeable results. Others are referred as "addicts" with the implication that they are untreatable because of their condition. There were four "alcoholics" and two patients diagnosed as "chronic schizophrenics" in my series (Chessick 1966) who were referred with the advice that they be put permanently in the state hospital.

I have previously designated this group of patients as borderline patients, because they seem to lie on the periphery of psychiatry, on the periphery of society, and on the periphery of penology. Some of them have been in and out of prisons as well as mental hospitals and have had repeated brushes with the police for various reasons.

It is very difficult to place any of these patients in a solid diagnostic category. That is to say, all of them show at various times the preponderance of a variety of defenses which would cause the diagnosis to shift, sometimes from day to day, if diagnosis is to be based on the predominance of any particular type of symptomatology.

Broadly speaking, the patients can be categorized into two major groups, but there is considerable overlap. The first group is what has been referred to as "borderline" or "panneurotic" cases by a variety of authors. These patients show various often bizarre and puzzling neurotic and psychosomatic symptoms. At times they are frankly delusional and psychotic whereas at other times they are quite lucid and show considerable potential to function. At the same time there is a certain peculiar stability to these patients. They shift from symptom group to symptom group without suffering a prolonged frank psychotic breakdown.

In the second group are the patients using primarily alloplastic defenses and presenting a variety of sociopathic symptoms, the most predominant of which is of some sort of addicting disorder.

At various times all of the patients in this second group, to the despair of their physicians and the panic of their families, consume large quantities of substances or combinations of substances, including opiates, barbiturates, marijuana, methyprylon (Noludar), mebrobamate, hydroxyzine (Atarax), mescaline, alcohol, amphetamine, and food. At other times, however, there is complete or almost complete abstention.

Certain physical and psychic symptoms such as aches and pains, including gnawing abdominal pains, insomnia, anxiety attacks, epileptiform seizures, tics and twitchings, and depression, periodically build up and are followed by an explosion of hyper-ingestion in which the patient is functionally paralyzed and concentrates all his energy on a compulsive "stuffing in" of various substances while other activities cease. In a few patients, the substance hyperingested is always the same, but in most patients it varies with the episode. During these times, the patients are referred with the diagnosis of being "addicts" or "alcoholics."

From the above description, it can be seen how intensely frustrating these types of patients can be. Either the patient is shifting back and forth between a puzzling variety of neurotic and psychosomatic symptoms with occasional lapses into frank psychotic delusional states, or he is shifting back and forth into various sociopathic behavior forms with the additional complication of periodic hyperingestion.

These rapid shifts, with all the excitement, storm, and panic they cause the patient and those around him, usually accompanied by either the missing of sessions, failure to pay the bill, or spending session after session in dealing with a particular group of symptoms that have just developed, render it extremely frustrating for the physician who is trying to engage in psychotherapeutic process with the patient. So many extraneous matters keep being introduced into the therapy that soon both the patient and the physician agree that they are not getting anywhere. There is, typically, an increasing exasperation on the part of the therapist as well as a developing barrage of complaints about the treatment from the patient, which usually leads to an impasse and a referral either for chronic hospitalization or to a psychiatrist who is known to have had some experience with "addicts." At any rate, some excuse usually is given to get rid of the patient, although in many instances the patient is not genuinely interested in stopping treatment.

One unifying principle of the group is the chaos of their lives.

This chaos can be produced by simply slowly or suddenly doing nothing! Those around the patient correspondingly become aware that the whole structure of his life is falling apart, and the most complex and excited reactions take place, often with the patient sitting calmly in the center of the storm (see Kazan 1967). Chaos can also be produced either by dramatic acting out, addiction episodes, or by the appearance and fluctuation of a variety of puzzling neurotic and psychosomatic symptoms.

Arieti (1955) has suggested the term "stormy personality," which covers some typical characteristics of the group. He writes:

> In their attempts to gain parental approval and love, and to avoid disapproval, they try all types of attitudes, and all of them to an extreme degree. . . . These patients often live in an atmosphere of catastrophe and doom. On the other hand they show an extreme resiliency, and seem able to recover strength, spirit and good humor easily.

The patients (see Chapter 11) are often overwhelmed by a sense of restlessness, boredom, and despair over the "meaninglessness" of life. They verbalize about this at great length. Antoine Roquentin, the hero of Sartre's *Nausea* (1964), illustrates this oppressive sense of boredom and preoccupation with the meaninglessness of the world. The patients complain of a sense of detachment from people and the stream of life, portrayed with brilliance by Camus (1957) in *The Stranger.*

The theoretical understanding of the borderline patient and the differentiation of these patients from other conditions is extremely difficult and at our present state of knowledge it remains an unsolved problem. Several papers have appeared, in addition to Grinker's book, all attempting to delineate the borderline condition, but although many points of view are represented, the concept remains hazy.

An important reason for this haziness is the great need for better agreement and understanding about primary-process thinking and of the primitive ego functions. Schafer's book (1968) is a welcome recent contribution to clarification and differentiation of the current terminology used to describe these primitive processes.

Another important aspect to understanding the borderline patient and to differentiating this condition from others lies in the peculiar nature of the object relations of these patients. For example, the central theme of Modell's work (1968) is that "the acceptance of painful reality rests upon the same ego structures that permit the acceptance of the separateness of objects." Good mothering in the first year or two of life permits the core of a positive sense of identity.

> This core permits the partial relinquishment of instinctual demands upon the object and in turn permits the partial acceptance of the separateness of objects. It is this process upon which reality testing hinges.

Odier's book (1956), a major contribution, deals at length with the subject of "magic, omnipotence, and anxiety," as Modell calls it. Odier emphasizes the role of anxiety, which he maintains is directly proportional to the amount of insecurity in early childhood, in producing regression to the prelogical stage of infantile thinking, so prominent in certain neurotic symptoms such as nightmares and phobias. He goes so far as to delineate what might be called a "hang-up" on the road to the development of normal object relations, the "neurosis of abandonment."

Odier develops the problem of excess childhood or infantile anxiety at length, and discusses the kind of prelogical and magical thinking that arises from it. A wealth of clinical material is presented. Odier's line of reasoning will now be traced.

In the emotional "absence" of the mother, a sense of helplessness and insecurity develops in the baby, accompanied by severe anxiety and an attempt to deal with it through magic or prelogical thinking. If this is a prolonged situation we have what Odier calls the "syndrome of ego dysfunction," the counterpart of Modell's lack of a "core of a positive sense of identity." The magic thinking involves either objectification of the fear—"whatever threatens me is wicked and whatever protects me is good," objectification of anger—toward animistic malevolent objects as chosen, and identification with the aggressor. The "objectification" is the magical defense—placing the anxiety and fear and anger *outside* of the psyche onto external objects, as in phobias, or onto fantasy objects as in nightmares or religion.

In the "neurosis of abandonment" the anxiety is objectified onto a human being instead of a cosmic image or a transitional object—who is then given the power of creating or abolishing abandonment or insecurity and helplessness. This individual is seen as all-powerful, sometimes benevolent and sometimes malevolent. The person with this neurosis, termed "the abandonee" by Odier, has a "blindness in the logic of interpersonal relations," which is the same concept that Modell is talking about.

The behavior of the "abandonee" is then discussed in detail by Odier, and is typical of clinical descriptions of object relations of borderline patients. The oscillation between love and hate, security and insecurity, dependency and paranoia, and the rapid transitions from euphoria to depression all as a function of the minor provocations or reassurances from the chosen objects are absolutely characteristic.

There is substantial agreement between Modell and Odier. More attention is necessary to the details of magical thinking and to how, as Modell puts it, an "absence of intuitive mothering" leads to such phenomena as "negative omnipotence."

Modell directly discusses borderline patients. His description of their absence of a sense of "beloved self" is important and a great clinical problem. His discussion of their object relations in terms of Buber's comparison of "I-it" and "I-thou," and his concept of the schizoid patient as taking himself as a transitional object or wrapping himself in a "magical cocoon" are valuable contributions.

Various attempts have been made to characterize and distinguish this group of patients from the psychodynamic point of view without much success. Kernberg (1967, 1968) makes an exhaustive study of the characteristics of these patients and a careful comparison with other disorders. He prefers the term "borderline personality organization" for this group, and calls attention to certain typical features. These are, for example, a lack of anxiety tolerance, lack of impulse control, and lack of developed sublimatory channels.

It is most important to note that oral aggression plays a crucial role in the psychodynamics, and that there is a premature development of oedipal conflicts as an attempt to escape from the oral rage, with a subsequent condensation of pregenital and genital conflicts. Experience from the present author's series of cases has confirmed these findings. In addition, Kernberg points out:

> Any situation which would normally develop into a deeper interpersonal relationship reveals the incapacity of these patients to really feel or empathize with another person, the unrealistic distortion of other people, and the protective shallowness of their emotional relationships.

He is also aware of their "pathology of internalized object relationships," as he calls it, and "an intensification and pathological fixation of splitting processes" in the ego functions of these patients.

From the point of view of the therapist, clear-cut distinctions between "character disorder," "borderline schizophrenia," or borderline patients are not as important as some understanding of the nature of the damage to the ego structure. Blos (1962) notes:

> In the treatment of these cases one has to go back to the pregenital phases: to oral dependency and oral aggression, and to the vicissitudes of "basic trust." Clinically we recognize the defectiveness of the synthetic function of the ego and the preambivalent aggression directed at object and self-representations in the persistent defectiveness of object constancy with ensuing affective and cognitive disturbances.

Turning now to the treatment of the borderline patient, empathic perception of the restricted ego functions and of the deep emptiness of these patients as a consequence of severe damage to the mother-child symbiosis in the first year of life enable the therapist to set limits and maintain an investigative attitude in spite of a bombardment of provocations. If the therapist is reasonable, has a healthy self-esteem, and is consistent and determined, therapy does get started, even though it sometimes appears impossible at first. The other essential ingredient to getting the patient into treatment is proper interpretation, again based on empathic perception. This is not hard at the beginning, as it usually centers around the patient's emptiness and loneliness.

A similar view is presented in much more detailed fashion by Little (1966). She speaks of patients with "psychotic anxieties" regarding annihilation, existence itself, and identity. She sees the analyst as supplying a "protective shield" or supplementary ego at first, which he can then gradually withdraw as the unbearable existential conflicts are worked through, and proceed into classical analysis. In a carefully reasoned paper she presents three views of how to deal with those patients mired in the preverbal dread of loneliness, emptiness, and isolation. Her position is to give a set of good-mothering experiences first; verbal interpretations cannot be used before this is supplied. She illustrates her point from her case material.

The resonance that is set up in the empathic relationship between the unconscious of the patient and the unconscious of the therapist has important resemblances to the early mother-child symbiosis. There is mutual fusing of ego boundaries and mutual exchange on a primitive, often nonverbal, level. The patient experiences important gratification from this process.

In the successful empathic situation, just as in a successful early mother-child symbiosis, a feeling of confidence develops in the patient. Confidence often permits a cementing of the therapeutic relationship even though the therapist makes errors that in a less empathic situation might lead to the breakup of the treatment.

Some psychoanalysts argue that even in the psychoanalytic

situation, where the "real" object relationship (Tarachow 1963) between the therapist and patient is minimized to the greatest possible degree, gratification through the empathic process is present and exerts an important healing force. For example, Menninger feels that when there is consistent empathy coming from the therapist, it sometimes calls forth in the patient a natural and realistic feeling of love or affection for the therapist. He writes (1958):

> It is a simple matter for the analyst to defend himself against the impact of these passions by discounting the patient's love as "not real." We should not forget, however, Freud's (1915) warning that "one has no right to dispute the genuine nature of the love which makes its appearance in the course of analytic treatment. However lacking in normality it may seem to be, this quality is sufficiently explained when we remember that the condition of being in love in ordinary life outside analysis is also more like abnormal than normal phenomena."

Menninger's implication is that acceptance of this love by the therapist, without trying to defend by ascribing it all to transference—even though it has many transference aspects which the therapist may or may not choose to ignore—may be an important experience in the patient's life.

At any rate, certainly in the psychotherapy of borderline schizophrenics, and in most supportive psychotherapy, a positive response to the genuine and human aspects of the therapist must be considered useful in producing the most effective atmosphere for the processes of growth, maturation, working through of insight, and indentification with the therapist. Even an identification with the capacity of the therapist to empathize is considered of value.

It might be argued that the primitive gratification experienced by the borderline patient in the empathic situation provides a freeing of energies that become available for the development of object love. In severely deprived patients, the generation and release of such feelings is extremely difficult, and takes a very long time. If there has been at least one such give-and-take love experience in early childhood—with a grandmother or a maid, for example—the prognosis is better, for this relationship can be used as a prototype, as well as an example of the rewards of being able to love.

The release of the universal, vital biologic urge and capacity to love, through a study of the situation that arises in response to consistent empathy in the therapist, can be quite helpful and rewarding to the patient. The interpersonal rewards that accrue as this capacity grows, can provide, along with hope, the major motivating forces for psychotherapeutic work.

The term "love" is a lay term and must be used cautiously. Perhaps it suggests to some too great an intensity and they would prefer such terms as "affection" or "respect," but this seems to depend on the personal preference of the therapist. Freud did not hesitate to use this term in a similar carefully defined context, as he has been quoted above and in his famous paper on *Some Character Types Met with in Psycho-Analytic Work* (1916), in which he wrote:

> . . . let us say that the physician in his educative work makes use of one of the components of love. In this work of after-education, he probably does no more than repeat the process which first of all made training of any kind possible. By the side of the necessities of existence, love is the great teacher; and it is by his love for those nearest him that the incomplete human being is induced to respect the decrees of necessity and to spare himself the punishment attendant on any infringement of it.

Furthermore, there must be a freedom of expression of emotion with the patient. The therapist cannot hide behind a professional mask but must be prepared to engage emotionally with the patient from the very beginning. This usually involves expressing anger at the patient which, if it is justifiable and expressed in a civilized way, can be quite helpful to the patient (and therapist), but it also can involve the expression of esteem and encouragement. As the intensity of the symbiosis heats up, enthusiasm and even affection are verbally expressed. For a symbiosis is what forms—the patient becomes "wrapped up" in the therapist—and the healthy therapist is able to offer himself as a "real object."

Tarachow (1963) speaks of this as the therapist's intruding himself into the life of the patient and staying there. He feels that when this takes place the therapist and patient have entered each other's lives as "real, serving as infantile objects to each other." Thus the therapist "uses himself as a building block in the oft-times jerry-built structure of defenses the patient has erected." However, no further detailed discussion is offered by Tarachow of just how the therapist and patient become "infantile objects" to each other.

In Chapter 9, Freud's (1923) statement that "the ego is a precipitate of abandoned object-cathexes" was quoted and discussed. The introjects can assist or impede ego development and the early introjects have a crucial bearing on how a person handles problems and on his sense of identity. Giovacchini (1967) points out that the child initially internalizes from his parents not only values and limits as in superego formation, but styles and techniques required to solve the problems of routine living. When he forms an introject of a parent he includes many elements of the relationship that involve methods of mastery. As Giovacchini (1967a) describes it, the inquiring but anxiety-free, consistent, and calm attitude of the therapist is "introjected" into the patient, enabling the development of an observing ego that can deal with malignant introjects.

However, introjection involves more than swallowing in an "attitude"—it involves in fantasy the swallowing of the whole or at least a part of a human being (Schafer 1968). Therefore, the basic deep feeling that the therapist has for the patient is swallowed in along with his attitude; if this feeling is primarily warm (it is always of course to some extent ambivalent) it will reinforce the therapy process vastly.

The initial and basic repair that has to go on in patients of this nature is the correction of a preverbal disaster. This repair takes place extremely slowly and is characterized by often taking place in spite of what is verbally going on between the patient and the therapist. Signs that it is taking place can be watched for in the therapy. For example, a most characteristic sign is the increase of ego span. A patient who would explode into a variety of symptoms upon frustration shows a longer and longer period of frustration tolerance. Sometimes the patient will notice this and report it. Thus, if the frustration tolerance had previously been a day, now the patient can wait a week for an important letter, or for a misplaced salary check, or the like, without developing characteristic symptoms.

When questioned closely as to why this sort of improvement has taken place, the patients usually can give only vague answers that seem to relate to being "wrapped up in the therapist." A therapist-patient symbiosis gradually is established in which the patient develops an almost "animal faith" (in the sense that this term is used by Santayana [1955]) in the consistency, honesty, determination, and, above all, the reliability of the therapist.

It almost goes without saying that the demands made on the therapist by such patients are tremendous. They require the therapist to avoid acting-out over years of intensive therapy in which the utmost tests are put to him to see if he can withstand what the patient has to offer. Such incidents as the therapist's canceling or coming late to appointments, mistakes in time of an appointment, broken promises, vacations, and even scientific meetings become major items for discussion in the therapy and there is a continuous scrutiny by the patient to see whether these everyday matters cannot be attributed to a basic dislike that the therapist has for the patient.

A therapeutic contract is developed in the face of a myriad of disruptive factors, based on the development of what has been described as a "locked-in symbiosis" (Chessick 1966). This symbiosis is a consequence of the healthy therapist offering a part of himself as a "real object" to the patient for the purposes of introjection. It is a symbiosis because the therapist must in some way be gratifying his own needs through this relationship, or he would prohibit it. It is a locked-in symbiosis out of the desperate inner emptiness of the patient, who, once he can be encouraged to clamp down like a bulldog on the therapist, will not let go if the object is a healthy one.

After some months or even some years of this relationship, the patient hopefully gradually swings around from oscillating psychiatric and psychosomatic symptoms and various kinds of bizarre acting out, to resembling more and more what we see in an ordinary psychotherapy situation. The therapist at that point begins to shift roles bit by bit toward a more neutral stance, with the aim of eliciting the basic early narcissistic fantasies that the patient has lived around. However, this can be done only after there has been sufficient locking in of the symbiosis between therapist and patient so that the patient can withstand the frustrations and anxieties involved in the uncovering of what are usually their pet and secret consolation narcissistic fantasies.

Again and again in their superficial and glib way, these patients present a variety of narcissistic aspirations that often stand in stark contrast to what they have accomplished. Direct assault on these narcissistic aspirations will usually lead to a breakup of the therapy because the patient has assumed these narcissistic fantasies as a consolation for his deep feelings of worthlessness and unlovableness, and so until these deep feelings are attenuated by the symbiosis with the therapist, he needs the fantasies desperately. In essence, the patient must as a first step replace the consolation narcissistic fantasies with an object relationship to the therapist.

Genuine improvement in object relations can only begin with such patients when these narcissistic fantasies have been uncovered and given up and the patients recognize that they can get on in the world without them, but to get to this point sometimes requires a very long period of relationship therapy. Clinical evidence of such improvement appears in such areas as showing greater ability to empathize with others, greater consideration for the feelings of others, development of closer and more mature relationships with family and friends, and the appearance of interest and concern for community problems.

Because of the psychodynamics of these borderline people, the therapist soon finds himself facing a "crucial dilemma" (Chessick 1968) regarding the choice from session to session between staying with a strict "technique" of psychotherapy and following an "inner attitude," which may even at times lead to temporary abandonment of previously learned techniques of psychotherapy. In the literature, Giovacchini (1967a) has argued for remaining strictly with "technique" whereas Nacht (1962, 1963) has emphasized the intuitive factors.

Watching neophyte therapists, it is easy to show that, for them, hiding behind rigid adherence to technique or rules of treatment constitutes a defense against feeling the anxiety engendered in them by the massive pregenital strivings of borderline patients. Analogous to this is society's tendency to treat such people with rigid rules, as, for example, "The army will make a man out of him."

Dangers in allowing an intuitive approach to such patients are also present, in that the therapist must genuinely know himself and not engage in countertransference acting-out. These patients are eager to act out or "act in" in the therapy, and they pose a threat to the neophyte for that reason also.

The key factor producing improvement is the therapist's empathic grasp of how the patient perceives and how he feels—and the therapist's ability to respond emotionally to this without predominantly using the patient for his own needs. In a similar fashion, the therapist must be able to draw away and permit "individuation" at the proper time.

Careful study of case material shows that it is actually possible to keep a "secondary process" check on what is going on and so avoid a wild and disorganized therapy. The more thoroughly understood the patient is, the more accurately it is possible to know whether our emotional interaction with the patient is "on the beam" from session to session. Improvement in the patient appears to be directly related to this emotional interaction and to the degree to which it is consistently genuine, "on the beam," and originates from a healthy and positive "deep inner attitude" of the therapist.

Lipshutz (1955) has already described two important characteristic manifestations that the transference takes in borderline patients. These involve, first, the customary intense and uninhibited expression of transference wishes early in the therapy and, second, the common appearance of a "third person" toward whom these transference feelings are later transmitted.

It is essentially the reduced strength of the ego that forces these patients to resolve the conflict by a shift to the third person. In my experience, considerable acting out with this third person may unfortunately occur before the patient can finally be persuaded that this is really a shift of fantasies away from the therapy and a draining out of affects that belong in the therapy situation.

Another type of transference problem encountered in borderline cases is what has been described as the "erotized" transference by Rapaport (1956). Such transference may, for example, appear as a stormy demand for genital contact with the therapist from the patient of the opposite sex. If this is rejected the patient claims deep hurt and humiliation. Repeated interpretations are not accepted and the patient persists. Rapaport suggests:

> Erotization is what the patient wants to make (of the analytic situation) under pressure of the repetition compulsion, while a corrective emotional experience is what the analyst tries to give to the patient by acting differently from the pathogenic parent. This is accomplished by constant reality testing and by keeping the tenuous balance between allowing the patient to believe that one is sincerely interested in him and has full confidence in his capacity to act effectively and in a mature manner, and at the same time discouraging any assumption that one has a stake in his therapeutic success.

In summary, this chapter has reviewed the problem of the borderline patient and the special difficulties he presents to the therapist, as an illustration of the many important factors involved in psychotherapy as described in this book. The most common erroneous responses to these difficult patients are attempts to directly minister to the patient's needs or adopting too detached and analytic an approach. If one can successfully walk a tightrope between these two horns of the therapist's "crucial dilemma" in the treatment of borderline patients, the patient is able to introject the warm inner attitude of the therapist toward him, develop better ego-adaptative techniques, and use a calm investigative atmosphere in which to examine himself.

All of these provide the tools to make a gradual modification in the basic malevolent introjects and thereby produce a genuine change in the patient in the direction of cure. The evidence for these contentions comes from the intensive long-term treatment by the author of 18 borderline patients over the past ten years and from his observations of neophyte therapists attempting to treat such patients under the author's supervision.

13

Learning About Psychotherapy

It has never been satisfactorily demonstrated that didactic courses in psychotherapy can really help teach a person how to do psychotherapy. There are three generally accepted ways of teaching psychotherapy—individual supervision, case seminars, and reading—either alone or in seminars. Individual supervision has the best potential, depending on the supervisor. In practice, supervisors are often chosen more because of either their availability or reputation rather than for their ability. Thus the supervisory staff often consists to a substantial extent of recently graduated psychotherapists who still have open time and are augmenting their income by teaching, and a few "shining lights," who are recruited by their reputation and who often generously donate their time to the program. Many experienced, capable, and valuable supervisors are lost because their time is simply filled up with private practice and other interests, and little active effort is made to recruit them. The very best training programs develop a certain *esprit de corps*, which motivates graduated psychotherapists to identify with the program and keeps them coming back to do supervisory work long after they have to for financial reasons. This is the ideal situation.

The problems of individual supervision and seminars are legion in number. There is no agreement on how to maximize the effectiveness of individual supervision (Tischler 1968). The literature abounds with conflicting discussions about this problem. Also, in order to benefit from individual supervision, the trainee must have certain innate capacities and sufficient mental health to at least enable him to listen to the patient and supervisor in spite of his anxiety (Fleming and Benedek 1964). In fact, it is absolutely inconceivable that anyone except the most extraordinarily talented individual could develop into a successful psychotherapist without first undergoing intensive long-term psychotherapy himself.

Individual supervision, as sometimes not recognized by either neophyte or supervisor, is a situation often fraught with anxiety for many reasons. In addition to the interpersonal interaction between trainee and supervisor, with all that this entails, Tischler (1968) and others have pointed out the frequent discrepancy between the goals of the supervisor and the goals of the neophyte in supervision. Those who practice psychotherapy are well aware of the chaos that can result when a discrepancy in goals between patient and therapist exists. A similar problem faces the supervisor and the trainee.

Certain basic assumptions underlying individual supervision have never been challenged or studied in detail. For example, can the resident accomplish a substantial change in his professional self under supervision without simultaneously in psychotherapy changing his personal self? What is the relationship of ego-systems constituting the "professional self" and those constituting the "personal self"? Furthermore, some supervisors assume a prior commitment in the resident to dynamic psychiatry and psychotherapy, whereas the resident is struggling with just such a commitment. This profound problem is often overlooked because of the exigencies of time, or the resident's fear of bringing up the matter to a supervisor who is obviously deeply involved in dynamic psychiatry.

It is tempting to go on and on about problems of individual supervision. For example, one factor that has been ignored in the literature is boredom of the supervisor. To avoid boredom in going through six-month periods of supervision with student after student over many years, careful provision must be made. Otherwise the boredom of the supervisor comes across to the student as a deficiency in object relationships and a similar boredom is transferred from student psychotherapist to patient with very unfortunate results for the psychotherapy.

The second generally accepted way of teaching psychotherapy is the "seminar." This technique has come under considerable recent criticism and has many serious defects. For example, Halmos (1966) discusses the paradox of the "faith in shortcuts and expediencies." The psychoanalytically oriented teacher recognizes that "intellectual insight" and direct didactic instruction are very poor methods indeed to bring about change in people. Yet our seminars are all based on the assumption that such didactic instruction, "spoon-fed" for the most part, will bring about a change in the "professional self" of the student. Here is an exciting area for research.

Ekstein and Wallerstein (1958) point out that teaching methods based on information-giving—"the authoritative transmission of technical advice"—may actually be detrimental since they tend to be dominated by the supervisor's way of doing things rather than by evoking the professional self of the student.

One of the few studies available of a less authoritative type of seminar, the so-called "continuous case conference," carried out by Guiora *et al.* (1967), indicates it to be a total failure as a learning experience. Guiora's report is overly pessimistic but again the whole matter has been very poorly explored. A deeper objection to any seminar on psychotherapy comes from the question whether a process such as psychotherapy, which is only in part—and perhaps only in small part—intellectual, can be studied intellectually without losing sight of the really important aspects.

The gloomy fact must be faced that anyone attempting to undertake the teaching of psychotherapy, whether by individual supervision or by seminar, is setting out on almost totally uncharted waters with little but instinct to guide him. This is another aspect of the "faith of the counsellors" as Halmos (1966) describes it. Unfortunately, many teachers follow the precept of Galbraith (1958): "It is a far, far better thing to have a firm anchor in nonsense than to put out on the troubled seas of thought."

The advantages of the seminar method mainly revolve around the problem the neophyte has with identification, commitment to dynamic psychiatry, and the development of his professional identity; for example, as a psychiatrist doing psychotherapy—if he ever develops such an identity (many residents in psychiatry never do).

The skilled seminar leader takes advantage of the dilution factor of a seminar, that is, the seminar is more like a class, more like what the student is used to in his background, and it has "safety in numbers." Consequently there is less intense interpersonal anxiety at least when the student is not directly "presenting" the case or literary material. It is obvious that the skilled seminar leader must exert constant pressure to prevent the group from tormenting the student "presenting" the case or literary material; there are many reasons both in individual and group dynamics why this tends to occur. Constant focus on the alliance of the group and the use of the presentation as a teaching experience, analogous to the recommendations of Greenson (1965) on maintaining the therapeutic alliance, are necessary from the seminar leader.

Furthermore, in the seminar, the pressure to identify is less; there is less of an anxiety-driven tendency to introject the seminar leader lock, stock and barrel, except in the most disturbed students who are overwhelmed by anxiety in the whole teaching situation. This affords the student a chance to look the seminar leader over and perhaps borrow bits and pieces of him but also to reject parts of him that are not compatible with the student's personal style.

Only the most unenlightened supervisor would expect the student to pattern his therapeutic identity on a style foreign to the student's personality; the best we hope for are partial identifications and corrections, which we hope can go on if the anxiety is not overwhelmingly intense. For example, some residents in psychiatry can even choose against ever doing any uncovering psychotherapy at all in this situation, for the seminar can allow enough interpersonal distance so the resident does not have to feel guilty if he does not develop an intense commitment to what the supervisor wants to spend his life doing.

For clinical work, the prediction seminar has been developed by the present author (1969) in an attempt to maximize the advantages of the seminar method of teaching and to gear the seminar as much as possible to the needs of the resident or neophyte in psychotherapy.

Ford (1963) discusses the anxieties and the problems in development of the resident in psychiatry. He points out that "the actual control mechanism of the psychiatrist's personality—his perceptual ego—is under constant probing and provocation from the anxious energy transferred by his patient."

Ornstein (1968) has reviewed the entire concept of training and education for psychotherapy from the point of view that emphasizes the therapist's use of himself as the primary instrument of diagnosis and treatment. The neophyte must develop the "basic skills" of "observation, evocative listening, empathy, intuition, and introspection" in the therapeutic encounter with the patient. This must be at the basis of all training and education for psychiatrists and psychotherapists.

Schwartz and Abel (1955) argue that there is no substitute in the teaching of psychotherapy for a clinical orientation in conferences, seminars, and case supervision. Supervisor selection, however, is a much more serious problem than previously anticipated. They note, for example, that "The tradition that an experienced and even successful psychoanalyst is automatically a good teacher or supervisor is not corroborated by experience." It is beyond the scope of this chapter to discuss in detail what makes a good teacher or supervisor, but certain remarks are in order.

Because of his feeling of emptiness and void, as Sharaf and Levinson (1964) point out, the resident in psychiatry is looking for "a magical figure in a fantasy of future omnipotence." This poses a danger to the resident from a seminar supervisor whose narcissistic and omnipotent infantile fantasies have not been worked through in his own treatment. The seminar can then be used as a source of reassurance for the supervisor for his own omnipotent fantasies and pretense at either "omniscience" or "omnisentience," as Sharaf and Levinson (1964) call it. The resident is then presented with the unconscious message: Be like me because it reassures me that I am omnipotent and I will reward you by transferring my omnipotence to you. Schwartz and Abel (1955) point out that the best protection against problems of this nature, besides personal therapy of the supervisor, is the existence within each training program of a regular training and exchange-of-ideas seminar for supervisors. In my experience, this has been *very* difficult to arrange, but when it occurs it is quite worthwhile.

What should the student of psychotherapy read either in a seminar or on his own? Out of the vast multiplicity of books it is necessary to make some very stringent choices or the beginner will be overwhelmed. It is also necessary to develop systematic reading habits and a three-year reading program in order to avoid becoming hopelessly lost in the more advanced texts. Keeping carefully in mind the danger of the "faith in shortcuts and expediencies," it is still necessary for a training program in psychotherapy to have a continuous seminar for journal articles and a continuous seminar for books running throughout the program. The journal articles are usually chosen as a function of the seminar leader's interests, and often include current articles of interest.

However, as is consistent with the theme of this book, a certain body of outstanding literature on psychotherapy has developed that forms required reading for the would-be psychotherapist. I will now present an annotated bibliography based on my viewpoints on what this literature ought to contain, although it is obvious that various substitutions and corrections would be perfectly reasonable depending on the therapeutic orientation of the seminar leader. However, omission of any book on *psychotherapy* from the discussion to follow means that for various reasons I consider it to be unsuitable for training psychotherapists.

All reading on psychotherapy is pointless unless the reader *first* has a thorough grounding in the basic humanities and in human history. No current individual human problems can be understood without humanistic and historical perspective. Therefore, I insist that the beginning reading seminar contain such books as selections from the Bible (especially the Book of Job, Ecclesiastes, and Proverbs), the Greek tragedies (available in an excellent edition from the University of Chicago Press), Homer (especially the Fitzgerald translation of *The Odyssey*), Plutarch (Modern Library edition), Dante—especially the *Purgatorio*, and the first part of Gibbon. A variety of plays should be read, including the tragedies of Shakespeare, Ibsen's *Hedda Gabler*, O'Neill's *Long Day's Journey Into Night*, and others the seminar leader chooses. These should be studied carefully and discussed, not simply skimmed over for the plot as nonscholars often tend to do.

The seminar leader should encourage the reading of a variety of novels that deal magnificently with important themes of psychodynamics and family interaction such as *The Dream of the Red Chamber, Buddenbrooks, Look Homeward Angel, The Brothers Karamazov, Of Human Bondage, The Trial*, and of course many others. Barchilon (personal communication) has formalized the study of novels as a method of teaching psychodynamics and is currently writing a book on the subject, which should be most useful.

Some historical understanding of the development of our civilization, of science, and of psychiatry and psychotherapy is obviously mandatory. The first book to be assigned is *The Rise of the West* by McNeill (1963). This book contains a remarkable integration of historical fact, descriptions and explanations of principal religions and their development, charts and diagrams of the origin and development of political and religious institutions, and fine photographs of important works of art to demonstrate the relationship of historical change and artistic development. A true panorama of human endeavor unfolds itself to the reader and one is tempted to return to this book again and again.

In addition, the beginner should read at least the three outstanding paperback biographies of Claude Bernard by Olmsted (1961), Paracelsus by Pachter (1961) and Sigmund Freud by Jones (1963). At present there is no really good text on the history of psychiatry or psychotherapy. The scholarly but tediously written and overly detailed book by Zilboorg (1941) is the best of the lot. An outstanding example of good scholarly psychiatric historical writing is *Hysteria: The History of a Disease* by Veith (1965), and this should not be missed.

A second very important basic humanities text is by Levi (1959). In this book, Freud is put into juxtaposition with other geniuses of the modern world such as Bergson, Spengler, Einstein, and many others. It is well written and most worthwhile; it reviews all the major systems of modern thought. A further discussion of Freud's political and social thought by Roazen (1968) —which also serves as an excellent introduction to Freud's thought in general—has recently appeared and is highly recommended.

It is also obviously pointless to read anything about psychotherapy until one understands the basic diagnostic entities in psychiatry, how to do a diagnostic work-up, interviewing techniques, and elementary principles of psychodynamics and their operation in the mental apparatus. One may choose from a variety of good textbooks. A number of summarizing textbooks, such as Noyes and Kolb (1963), English and Finch (1957), or Redlich and Freedman (1967), are available.

The only book on adolescence that is a truly outstanding but very advanced "classic" on the subject is by Blos (1962). Lidz (1968) and Erickson (1950) on personality development should not be missed. Other important general books that are mandatory to a beginning program in psychotherapy are by Russell (1930), Fromm (1956), and Jung (1933). Also, two books that give an excellent overview of contrasting psychoanalytic theories are by Mullahy (1948) and Munroe (1955).

After these books have been studied thoroughly, the seminar can turn with ease to more specific aspects of psychodynamics. The case histories of Freud have become classics. Other works by Freud (e.g., 1915–1916, 1923, 1938) and Anna Freud (1946) are also classics. The discussions of the "As-If" personality or "The Imposter" in Deutsch (1965), of the psychodynamics of depression in Mendelson (1960), and of schizophrenia in Bleuler (1950), Bellak (1958), and Arieti (1955) are all of the utmost importance.

Let us turn now directly to books on psychotherapy. If the student has digested the readings for the first year as already discussed, he is ready to tackle the subject with a critical eye. We shall divide the readings into three sections: (1) basic books, (2) more advanced books, and (3) books on special problems in psychotherapy.

The basic books are of two kinds, either "cookbook" or general. Examples of the "cookbook" type are Wolberg (1954) and Colby (1951). I prefer the former, although it is much longer. The second edition appeared in 1967 in two volumes and can be read outside of a seminar since it is a clear and simple presentation. Colby contains some statements that are very controversial, such as, "If it is at all possible, use a couch." For the beginner's seminar, the two best general books available on psychotherapy are by Fromm-Reichmann (1950) and DeWald (1964), frequently quoted and sometimes criticized in the present book. The former is easier to read; the latter begins with an excellent review of psychodynamics. Two books by Masserman (1955, 1961) are often valuable as supplementary readings.

The seminar for neophyte psychotherapists should not overlook Friedman (1955) on *Martin Buber*, Frank (1961) on *Persuasion and Healing*, or Ruesch (1961) on *Therapeutic Communication*. If there is time, the selected papers of Fromm-Reichmann (1959), the first five chapters of Beier (1966) on covert communication in psychotherapy, and a stimulating text by Alexander (1956) provide outstanding material for discussion and deepening of one's understanding of psychotherapy.

More advanced books of really great value are few in number but supreme in their reward. They are all psychoanalytic texts, but are so well written that the student of psychoanalytically oriented psychotherapy will find them packed with valuable ideas and clinical material even though he is not practicing formal psychoanalysis. My favorite above all is Saul (1958), frequently quoted in the present book. Greenson (1968) is outstanding as an example of beautiful writing and presents many useful clinical examples. It is marred by a rather tedious pedantic tendency to make divisions and subdivisions in theoretical categories, but these can be taken lightly and the text serves as the finest written example I know of that describes, in many details, a psychoanalytically oriented psychotherapist in action with his patients.

Glover's (1955) book contains a classic section on the inexact interpretation; the rest can be omitted for our purposes. Fenichel (1941) and Stone (1961) are technical and difficult authors but they bring up a number of vital issues for the advanced psychotherapist. Menninger (1958) presents an excellent book to use for an advanced seminar. It contains an unusually vivid set of diagrams that are valuable in a discussion of what happens in psychotherapy and also some fuzzy and controversial thinking that is stimulating for discussion.

Books on special problems in psychotherapy include a number of very important ones that must not be missed after the neophyte has reviewed the basic texts mentioned above. Two classics are by Aichorn (1945) on delinquents and Reich (1949) on character analysis. Only the first two parts of Reich's book are worth reading, but they are most valuable. *The Psychoanalytic Reader*, edited by Fliess (1948), also contains some chapters by Reich on the same subject and other important papers as well.

Tarachow's (1963) book has achieved some popularity. He is a controversial "splitter," as defined in Chapter Three, and is best read for his clinical "pearls" on special problems in the psychotherapy of certain difficult disorders such as paranoid, acting-out, or suicidal patients. His work is essentially the transcript of resident seminars, and so lacks literary depth. Knight (1954) on the borderline patient has become a classic.

The psychotherapy of schizophrenia forms a major topic all by itself. It is mandatory to master the language of Harry Stack Sullivan in order to benefit from his extraordinary and unique insights into schizophrenia. Anyone who plans to work with schizophrenic or borderline patients will find it necessary to plow through *Conceptions of Modern Psychiatry* (1947) and *The Interpersonal Theory of Psychiatry* (1953) in order to learn Sullivan's approach thoroughly. The summary books previously mentioned (Mullahy 1948, Munroe 1955) cannot do justice to Sullivan—he must be read and appreciated in the original. If the reader is willing to put in the work, he is then prepared to benefit from Sullivan's *Clinical Studies in Psychiatry* (1956) and *Schizophrenia as a Human Process* (1962), from Hill's (1955) outstanding *Psycho-therapeutic Intervention in Schizophrenia,* from a rereading of Fromm-Reichmann (1950, 1959), and from the collected papers of Searles (1965), which form the most advanced of this group of readings. Brody and Redlich's (1952) collection of papers on the psychotherapy of schizophrenics is also outstanding.

Since most residency programs in psychiatry begin with the inpatient treatment of schizophrenics, it is wise to offer a seminar during the first year on this series of books, which are written in such a way that even without prior experience the neophyte can utilize them to gain an understanding of schizophrenia from a psychodynamic point of view.

Amazingly, there is almost nothing published on the teaching and learning of psychotherapy except for the unusual and outstanding book by Ekstein and Wallerstein (1958), which to my knowledge is now out of print.

In this chapter it may seem that a great many books have been reviewed and suggested. Although this appears to require a lot of reading, it is nothing in comparison to the tremendous number of books available. It is hoped, therefore, that this annotated bibliography can serve as a guide to seminar leaders and students by presenting an orderly progression of outstanding works for study.

In summary, this chapter has reviewed a variety of difficulties involved in didactic training in psychotherapy. The three traditional didactic methods are individual supervision, case seminars, and individual or seminar-directed reading. All methods have serious problems and limitations and their effectiveness remains poorly tested. An annotated bibliography is presented to guide seminar leaders and students to an orderly progression through the most valuable reading.

PART IV

Metapsychiatry

14

The Science of Psychotherapy

The argument as to whether psychotherapy is or is not a "science" has become tiresome and overworked. Perusal of the literature indicates that, for the most part, the argument is used for rhetorical purposes. Those authors who do not "like" psychotherapy, who are suspicious of it for personal reasons, or who are simply not psychologically minded and must have things to touch and count, all vehemently argue that psychotherapy is not a "science." Authors who practice or support psychotherapy maintain that it is indeed a "science."

Hidden behind all this rhetoric are the assumptions, first, that it is highly desirable or even indispensable that psychotherapy be a "science" and second, that the protagonist knows the meaning of the term "science." It is of course not difficult to argue that if "science" implies a body of knowledge that can supply us with the means to ameliorate or cure mental illness as it has done in other fields of medicine, it is highly desirable that psychotherapy approximate "science." The real confusion comes in the frequent misunderstanding of the meaning of "science."

Most authors still assume the old philosophical descriptions of science as being based on the procedure first of collecting empirical observations and then making "inductions" from these "facts." Modern philosophers have demolished this description of the method of science entirely.

Kuhn (1962) argues, for example, that "normal science" presupposes a conceptual and instrumental framework accepted without question by the entire scientific community. Crises within the normal work of science or through the introduction of new instrumentation occur from time to time and lead to a replacement of the current conceptual and instrumental framework—a scientific revolution.

Popper (1965) points out that actually in the development of science "observations and experiments play only the role of critical arguments." They play this role alongside other, nonobservational arguments. He writes:

> According to the theory of knowledge here outlined there are in the main only two ways in which theories may be superior to others: they may explain more; and they may be better tested—that is, they may be more fully and more critically discussed, in the light of all we know, of all the objections we can think of, and especially also in the light of observational or experimental tests which were designed with the aim of criticizing the theory.

In his view, knowledge proceeds by way of *conjectures* and *refutations*. Our scientific knowledge progresses by starting with unjustified anticipations, by guesses, by tentative solutions, that is, by *conjectures*. These conjectures are controlled by criticism, that is, by attempted *refutations*, which include severely critical tests. One can never prove that the conjectures are absolutely true, but:

> Criticism of our conjectures is of decisive importance: by bringing out our mistakes it makes us understand the difficulties of the problem which we are trying to solve. This is how

we become better acquainted with our problem, and able to propose more mature solutions; the very refutation of a theory is always a step forward that takes us nearer to the truth.

It follows that those theories that turn out to be highly resistant to our attempts at refutation or criticism at a certain moment of time constitute the science of the time. They are not, however, to be regarded as "truth." Science begins not with the collection of observations or invention of experiments but with the criticism of extant myths—with the critical discussion of myths and of magical techniques and practices. The scientific tradition passes on not only the myths but the criticism and the critical attitude toward them, and this critical attitude distinguishes the scientific from the prescientific.

Therefore, in contrast to the often erroneously held view, science does not consist of indubitable truth (*epistēmē*, Latin: *scientia*) or of technology (*technē*), but of opinions or conjectures (*doxai*), controlled by critical discussion as well as experimental technology. This will be discussed in greater detail below when we turn to Adler's recent theories.

Popper argues that a young scientist who hopes to make discoveries is badly advised if his teacher tells him to go around at random and observe. He advises, "Try to learn what people are discussing nowadays in science, find out where difficulties arise, and take an interest in disagreements. These are the questions which you should take up." We begin with the theoretical framework—not perhaps a very good one but one which works more or less—and use it by checking it over and by severely criticizing it. In this way we make progress.

The severe criticism can be of two kinds. First we have the rational discussion or "non-observational arguments." The present book serves as an example of this aspect of scientific investigation. Second, we have the critical experimental tests.

Popper puts the ideal way of deciding between theory t_1 and theory t_2 as follows: we can say that t_2 supersedes t_1 if :

1. t_2 makes more precise assertions than t_1, and these more precise assertions stand up to more precise tests.

2. t_2 takes account of and explains more facts than t_1.

3. t_2 describes the facts in more detail.

4. t_2 has passed tests that t_1 has failed to pass.

5. t_2 has suggested new experimental tests.

6. t_2 has unified or connected various hitherto unrelated problems.

This approach therefore provides criteria for "degrees of verisimilitude." Popper's views are the work of a lifetime and extremely well presented. His material contains tremendous stimulation of thought.

The present author would like to propose at this point the term *metapsychiatry.* The subject of metapsychiatry is the investigation of whether "knowledge" gained through psychotherapy such as "principles of psychodynamics" is knowledge at all, and, if so, in what sense. The scientific, artistic and philosophical aspects of psychotherapy all need to be clarified under the study of metapsychiatry. In metapsychiatry we try to determine (1) the position of psychotherapy in Western philosophical tradition, (2) to what extent psychotherapy can be said to be a "science" and to yield "scientific knowledge," and (3) to what extent it is philosophy or art. Clarification of these issues could save much needless rhetoric and argument. The term "metapsychiatry" should not be confused with the term "metapsychology," which has a totally different technical meaning and is a misnomer.

The remainder of this chapter will investigate the current scientific status of psychotherapy and serve as an introduction to metapsychiatry.

The first statements on metapsychiatry come from Popper, and they are not encouraging. He believes psychoanalysis is not a science and bases this on a very important distinction between science and pseudoscience. In fact the term "metapsychiatry" comes from Popper's use of the term "metascience." We know what a good scientific theory should be like even before it is tested. "It is this [meta-scientific] knowledge which makes it possible to speak of progress in science, and of a rational choice between theories."

It is easy to obtain confirmations or verifications for nearly every psychological theory. It is well known that "clinical observations" have been used to support every sort of theory of psychotherapy. A theory such as psychoanalysis, Popper maintains, is not refutable by any conceivable event. *Any* clinical observation can be explained by the theory and could never refute the theory. Therefore it is not scientific, for, "The criterion of the scientific status of a theory," writes Popper, "is its falsifiability or refutability, or testability."

Some theories are more testable than others. Those capable of being put to really critical empirical tests that could seriously refute the theory are defined as scientific. Popper calls this the "criterion of demarcation."

This book will not discuss Popper's contention that psychoanalysis (both Freudian and Adlerian) is "simply irrefutable" and therefore unscientific. What is of importance to our discussion of psychotherapy is that psychotherapy is obviously in between the clearly refutable and the clearly irrefutable. One cannot devise any clear and distinct experiments that would decisively prove that one psychotherapeutic approach was invariably better than another. Yet, as the fashion of this book demonstrates, it has become possible over the past fifty years to accumulate knowledge and understanding of what *not* to do in many psychotherapeutic situations, and violation of these precepts often leads to an awful chaos. This constitutes experimentation and refutability in the scientific sense.

The previous statement is one of the central contentions of this book. Although it arises primarily out of clinical experience, the trend in psychotherapy research has provided increasing support for it, as indicated, for example, in the recent exhaustive review of psychotherapy research by Strupp and Bergin (1969). They report:

> The isolation and manipulation of single variables is essential
> for advancing knowledge concerning the process of therapeu-

tic change. Moreover, it is becoming increasingly feasible to carry out such investigations without dependence on doctrinaire allegiances.

Thus, in psychotherapy we can meet Popper's contention that science is a procedure whose rationality consists in the fact that we learn from our mistakes. Furthermore, as the present book demonstrates, we have progressed over the years from a rather simplistic approach, to tackling problems of ever-increasing depth and complexity. Simultaneously it has become possible to offer psychotherapy to patients of ever-increasing depths of psychopathology such as the schizophrenic or the borderline patient. These patients were at one time considered inaccessible to psychotherapy.

The early Greek and Christian leaders were faced with the same situation the psychotherapist faces today—unhappy supplicants desperately in need of some way of relieving their minds of the misery of emotional disorder. Here is the problem of the psychotherapist ever since early Egyptian prayer ritual was prescribed for the cure of impotence in 3000 B.C.: trying somehow to evoke the development of an inner harmony in the individual that would at least permit some sort of realization of this individual's capacity for reason, love, and productive work.

The original therapeutic method of Breuer and Freud, that of hypnosis with catharsis during the hypnosis, has a very direct historical relationship to the ancient methods of treatment. Devising a method of free association was another step forward in the direction of therapy. The method removes to as great an extent as is possible the mystical noncontrollable elements of the relationship between the doctor and the patient. It changes the psychotherapist from a stage magician like Mesmer to a doctor engaged in controlled interpersonal relations with the patient and having as his goal the development of the patient toward maturity.

This was a brilliant advance in the field of psychiatry; it lifted psychiatry out of the realm of speculative mysticism, and made the material of the doctor-patient relationship amenable to the collection of facts for the purpose of the refutation of conjectures.

Freud was, above all else, a clinician. He scribbled his writings in the early hours of the morning and had little time for corrections. *This was because he was busy all day with patients.* And it was from this data of the doctor-patient relationship that Freud was able to draw his conclusions about human mental mechanisms.

Freud (1914) wrote:

> I was not subject to influence from any quarter; there was nothing to hustle me. I learnt to restrain speculative tendencies and to follow the unforgotten advice of my master Charcot—to look at the same things again and again until they themselves begin to speak.

The genius of Freud lies in his open-mindedness and absolute integrity, his willingness to examine the facts without any preconceived horrors, his insistence that the fundamental rules of empirical science be applied, and his ability to form far-reaching conjectures from the examination of facts.

Clinical experience comes not from knowing a lot of people or having years of experience in talking with people of all sorts and kinds, but from being repeatedly thrown into the situation of the psychotherapist. This situation originally faced Freud; he was the doctor expected to help, surrounded by supplicants, all of whom were under intense pressure from the misery of emotional disorder. *It is only when sitting in the interview room facing the psychiatric patient,* that the problems of psychotherapy become intense and vivid and the meaning of "clinical experience" becomes clear.

The great difficulties in psychotherapy and in understanding mental illness are not that psychoanalytic hypotheses are based on faith but that they are based on the examination of exceedingly complex clinical data, the interpersonal relationship between the patient and the doctor.

In our field two great barriers handicap our learning anything. The first of these might be termed the inexactness of the material. Work with human beings involves many as yet uncontrolled variables. This situation makes it most difficult to determine cause and effect by the classical method of science. However, in this day and age, with the advent of quantum physics and the development of statistical and experimental techniques for dealing with probability, this inexactness need not be a barrier that makes learning completely impossible.

The second great barrier to our learning might be termed our *unawareness* about the material, a barrier that, of course, overlaps the first. In the doctor-patient situation, we can never be entirely sure that we know what we are doing because the patient and the doctor are never aware of all the processes that are going on in them or between them.

It is the task of the future to devise increasingly better experimentation in the hope of providing clear refutations of different theories of psychotherapy. For the time being we can sidestep the problem by agreeing that psychotherapy is on the border between a clearly scientific body of knowledge on the one hand, and what Popper calls "philosophical" knowledge, on the other. It is simply *not* a clearcut distinction but fortunately, even if psychotherapy is not pure science, there are still some important criteria that can be used to criticize any psychotherapeutic theory, since it is a proposed solution to a set of problems.

We can ask, for example, if the theory solves the problem better than other theories. Has it merely shifted the problem? Is the solution simple and fruitful? Does it contradict other theories needed for solving other problems?

Probing further into metapsychiatry, let us begin with Mazlish (1968), who believes that psychotherapy has taken a decisive step from philosophical knowledge to scientific knowledge. He writes:

> . . . the differences between Nietzsche and Freud mark the decisive step in the advance from philosophy to science in the field of depth psychology. In the case of the Brunos, Mande-

villes, and Nietzsches we have philosophical (or theological) positions, arrived at by the method of intuition, with their confirmation or verification sought after either by the same method or by a form of faith. Opposed to this is the attempt at forming a "new science" by men like Galileo, Smith, and Freud.

To understand this more thoroughly it must be pointed out that there are *three* bodies of "knowledge." First we have "prescience," which consists of theories held by intuition or guesses and which does not include attempts at critical refutation. Second, we have "philosophical knowledge," which is demarcated from the third—"scientific knowledge"—by the existence or nonexistence of certain critical empirical tests that could decisively refute any given theory.

Psychotherapy has moved in the last fifty years from prescience to the border between philosophy and science. No experimentation is yet devised to refute decisively any broad areas of psychotherapeutic approach, but a body of clinical experience has been accumulated to refute a variety of approaches in more specific situations.

Adler (1965) points out that even philosophical knowledge is capable of being made meaningful and important. Therefore, even if one does not wish at this time to accept psychotherapy as "scientific," there are still certain criteria that must be satisfied if it is to be more than "mere opinion" or "prescientific." These criteria are the same as demanded by Adler for any philosophical knowledge.

What are the conditions that philosophical knowledge must meet in order to be worthy of respect? These are as follows:

1. It must be more than mere opinion or mythology. Adler makes certain vital distinctions, borrowed from Popper and the ancients, and of the greatest importance. He points out that the Greek ideal of mathematics and science has been *epistēmē*, which consists of certain, final, and incorrigible conclusions, having as their grounds, self-evident axioms (Greek: *nous*). Even mathemat-

ics does not really reach this ideal—in fact, there is no body of knowledge of this kind!

It does not follow that everything else is mere opinion. There is an area of "moderate" knowledge or *doxa* consisting of propositions that are (a) more or less testable by reference to evidence, (b) subject to rational criticism, and either (c) corrigible and rectifiable or (d) falsifiable. Understanding the difference between *doxa* or well-founded opinion and mere opinion is crucial to understanding the revolution between Bruno and Galileo or between Nietzsche and Freud.

2. The remainder of the conditions hinge on the first. Although the propositions of philosophical knowledge need not be provable in the absolute sense, they must be subject to falsification by appeal to the data of experience, thus permitting criteria of truth to exist in the field.

At this point Adler flatly disagrees with Popper's "criterion of demarcation" (see discussion above) and argues that the theories of philosophical knowledge are just as subject to experience as the theories of scientific knowledge. The experience he refers to is not from scientific experiment but from "the common experience of mankind." This is consistent with our previous discussion of the gradual accumulation of common clinical experiences among psychotherapists.

3. The examination of philosophical theories must be capable of being communicated and discussed by colleagues, that is, it must be capable of public examination and discussion.

Finally, there must be autonomous or unique or "first order" questions that are asked by any branch of "philosophical knowledge" that cannot be answered by any other discipline. The answers to these questions must not be too wildly removed from the common-sense world. It is clear, even from the first paragraphs of the present book, that psychotherapy does ask such "first-order" questions.

Adler also offers four interesting technical criteria for deciding among philosophical doctrines, the discussion of which is beyond the scope of this book; two criteria are logical and two are empirical.

In summary, we have seen how the question "Is psychotherapy scientific?" is really a very complicated one, often assuming an erroneous understanding of the term "science." The term "metapsychiatry" was introduced to cover the investigation of the scientific and artistic aspects of psychotherapy, and to locate psychotherapy in the Western philosophical tradition. Under Popper's conception of science as consisting of conjectures and refutations, and demarcated from philosophy by possessing the potential for crucial experimental refutation, psychotherapy lies on the border between scientific and philosophical knowledge. Although it has progressed like a science, proper crucial experiments have not been devised to refute whole theoretical approaches in psychotherapy. At the same time a body of clinical experience has accumulated that acts to refute approaches in specific situations, as the present text illustrates.

A broader but more controversial view would distinguish between science and philosophy only by the kind of experience used to refute theories. In science the crucial refutation comes from experiment; in philosophy, from the common experience of mankind. All this knowledge is essentially equivalent. None of it is absolutely true, but none can be classified as "mere opinion." The position of psychotherapy again seems to be a mixed one between science and philosophy, as these terms are defined in the discussion. The delineation of scientific and artistic and philosophical aspects of psychotherapy is a vital future task for metapsychiatry.

15

The Art of Psychotherapy

A tremendous amount of communication goes on during a psychotherapy session. On the nonverbal level it is always multiple, continuous, and changing at many levels with many different frequencies. On the verbal level the quantity of spoken words per minute varies of course with patients and with sessions, but also for any given quantity of spoken words, noises, and phrases, there are a number of varying levels of meanings and hence numerous communications being transmitted at one time. The change rate of these levels also differ, so two phrases may express two different topics at one level and the same topic at another level.

For those who are mathematically minded, the infinitude of constantly changing communications presented by the patient is immediately apparent. This is still more complicated in psychotherapy by the fact that a similar situation is presented by the therapist to the patient. What we end up with, therefore, is an intense interpersonal interaction in a contrived situation, with the exchange of numerous communications and responses at many levels and at times even self-contradictory among themselves.

This, on the operational level, is psychotherapy. The best way to be convinced of it is to watch psychotherapy through a two-way mirror with appropriate audio equipment. If this material is filmed and recorded, one can spend a lifetime analyzing one session for all levels of communications and responses. Many an unfinished research project on psychotherapy attests to this fact.

It is not to be concluded, as some have tried to do, that because of the infinitude of communications and responses, psychotherapy becomes meaningless and utterly unscientific. The only reasonable conclusion possible is that research on the psychotherapy process is an enormously complicated matter. However, one must admit that when dealing with such a multitude of stimuli from the patient it is impossible to delineate an exact scientific procedure that can be rigidly followed; psychotherapy, because of its intrinsic nature and the tremendous number of variables that are constantly present, can never be reduced to an exact science. Any model of psychotherapy, no matter how carefully designed, must by necessity be extremely oversimplified—much in the manner that early models of the atom were oversimplified by physicists.

Thus, certain aspects of psychotherapy, similar to the game of chess, can be sorted out and approached scientifically. But vast areas of the procedure entail a creative enterprise and in this sense psychotherapy becomes an art. It follows that we are dealing with a field that is partly a science and partly an art.

This leads to an anomalous situation for the person who is attempting to be a psychoanalytically oriented psychotherapist. He is caught between the "two cultures" that have been described by C. P. Snow (1963). If he is a sensitive and conscientious psychotherapist he will by training be a scientist, but by vocation be also partly an artist. Snow is by training a scientist and by vocation a writer. He describes how he lived among the scientists and among the writers and moved regularly from one group to the other, and how he came up with the concept of two cultures:

> I believe the intellectual life of the whole of western society is increasingly being split into two polar groups . . . literary intellectuals at one pole—at the other scientists. . . . Between

the two a gulf of mutual incomprehension—sometimes (particularly among the young) hostility and dislike, but most of all lack of understanding. They have a curious distorted image of each other. Their attitudes are so different that, even on the level of emotion, they can't find much common ground. . . . The nonscientists have a rooted impression that the scientists are shallowly optimistic, unaware of man's condition. On the other hand, the scientists believe that the literary intellectuals are totally lacking in foresight, peculiarly unconcerned with their brother men. . . . And so on.

The psychotherapist is very rapidly moving back and forth between the role of scientist and artist during the psychotherapy process itself. This requires a very solid sense of identity in the psychotherapist. He will be criticized by the scientist as performing an unscientific discipline. He will not be accepted by the artist because there are many aspects of his work that are scientific which restrict him in his creativity. These restrictions arise from the fact that psychotherapy is basically teleological, that is, it is being performed for the very specific end of relieving emotional suffering on the part of the patient. It is not an art for art's sake nor is the goal of the creation left completely up to the choice of the artist in this case. The result of the psychotherapy is judged not on the basis of esthetics but on the basis of relief of suffering that it can achieve.

Yet the task of confronting the psychoanalytically oriented psychotherapist is remarkably similar to the task confronting the artist in certain ways. Huxley (1963), for example, writes:

That is the task confronting every serious writer; for it is only by an unusual combination of purified words that our more private experiences in all their subtlety, their many-faceted richness, their unrepeated uniqueness can be, in some sort, re-created on the symbolic level and so made public and communicable. And even so, even at the best, how hopeless is the writer's task!

Picking the crucial themes out of the myriad of communications and interactions and presenting these back to the patient in an effective way combined with a proper sense of timing as to when the patient is ready for them constitutes the essential creative aspect of psychoanalytically oriented psychotherapy.

One notices psychiatrists reacting to this problem in a variety of different ways. For example, one group of psychiatrists steers completely away from the artistic aspects of psychotherapy and identifies firmly with the medical community. This group has been described as the "directive and organic therapists" by Hollingshead and Redlich (1958). They tend to give drugs, electric shock treatment, various kinds of somatic treatments, and advice. They wear white coats, go to medical meetings, and read a very special set of medical journals. They handle the patient physically, including the giving of minor treatment procedures and physical examinations. Their sessions with the patients are short and less frequent and there is a tendency to be convinced of an organic etiology to mental illness.

This variety of reaction is also present in certain types of psychologists, another significant professional group doing psychotherapy in the United States today. These psychologists follow certain rigid experimental schools and attempt to force psychotherapy to go along certain theoretical lines, hoping to keep the personal aspects to an absolute minimum. Their literature is replete with statistical studies of variables that are isolated out of the therapy process and makes very dull reading indeed.

Solutions such as these, which are equivalent to simply putting on blinders that filter through only what the therapist wishes to deal with, simply close the subject of psychotherapy at this point much as a discussion of religion can be firmly closed by one of the partners abruptly asserting a faith and refusing to admit a multitude of possibilities. The polar opposite but equally closed type of solution is found in the psychotherapist who adheres rigidly or dogmatically to a set of theories produced by some genius of days gone by. Such therapists will also see in the myriad of communications only what they wish to.

In the practice of psychoanalytically oriented psychotherapy as a creative discipline, however, it is hoped that a deeper and more profound attempt will be made to pick out crucial themes from the communications and interactions of the patient. This is an extremely difficult assignment, as we are increasingly aware of the powerful unconscious forces that propel the therapist to hear and communicate what makes him the least anxious. This was behind Freud's concept of trying to develop "evenly hovering attention" (see Harrison 1966) in which he hoped that a minimum of interference with listening would develop from the preoccupations and problems of the therapist, leaving him as free as possible to pick up basic themes that the patient was trying to communicate. Hence, the first and foremost task of the psychotherapist, as described by Fromm-Reichmann (1950), is to be able to listen.

The capacity to listen with evenly hovering attention is an extremely difficult one to teach and at least partly must be an inborn trait. There are certain people who are psychologically minded and are willing to suspend judgment and look and listen for deeper themes in communicated material while there are other persons who must deal only with superficial facts and simply cannot grasp underlying themes. This is in some ways a function of the capacity to feel empathy with another person. This capacity is in many ways similar to an artistic or creative ability.

These views are supported by such authorities as Wolberg (1954), Hill (1955), Alexander (1956), and Bromberg (1962). The ability to establish and to maintain a relationship with a patient is definitely a form of artistry. It is dependent on certain personality factors that some therapists are more highly endowed with than others. Theoretical knowledge is important, but the "aptitudes," as Alexander calls them, of intuition and empathic capacity, although not always reliable, are vital factors in establishing and maintaining a relationship. Personal therapy helps the therapist polish these and other vital factors, but cannot put them there if they are absent. Therefore, as is well known, we have some therapists who naturally engage in therapeutic communication even though much less formally trained than other therapists.

Hill emphasizes the multiple meanings of the word "treat," which include the meaning used by the artist when he describes the techniques used to grasp and understand a subject, and then translates his impression into a satisfactory portrayal of it. He compares "treatment" to the work of an architect, and points out that "The psychiatrist is in a definite sense an artist who works with a living medium toward creative ends."

Bromberg attempts to investigate in detail the "extratechnical" aspects of the psychotherapeutic relationship. He enumerates the factors of magical thinking, or "the artful (dramatic, nonverbal, stylistic) application of the healing technique," of nonverbal or preverbal symbolic patterns, and of certain features in the therapist that we have discussed under other headings.

In my opinion it is best to confine the notion of "artistic" factors in psychoanalytically oriented psychotherapy to certain creative, intuitive, or empathic features in the person of the therapist that cannot be taught or even formalized. To be "in tune" with one's own unconscious or the unconscious of others depends partly on one's state of ego-functioning and partly on this innate capacity. To pick out of the myriad of communication those "red threads" (Chapter 6) so emphasized by Saul (1958) that are vital in order to make each hour count is a creative art that can only partly be taught.

Formal training and study of the various factors discussed in the present work must be seen as necessary for the proper bending and channeling of this innate creative ability into a truly effective capacity to heal. Physicians showing this intuitive and empathic ability should be encouraged to have formal training as psychotherapists.

Without the capacity to empathize with another human being and enter into a feeling relationship with him at the deepest levels, a therapist is dangerously capable of doing harm; the patient, who is desperately reaching out, experiences this deficiency as a crushing rejection—which may make it impossible for another therapist ever to reach the patient. There are many examples of this in psychiatric literature.

The adequate training of capable and skilled therapists is shockingly absent in our culture. Much of the training goes on in a desultory fashion during psychiatric residencies, during which large bodies of factual knowledge must also be absorbed along with the burdens of multiple duties of hospital patient care.

Just because a physician finishes a psychiatric residency he is not necessarily qualified to do an adequate job of psychoanalytically oriented psychotherapy. Yet no distinction is made between those psychiatrists with adequate training in this area and those who are essentially untrained or unable to do psychotherapy.

It is to be hoped that the American Board Examination in Psychiatry will be modified to better explore the candidate's capacity to do psychotherapy or that a separate certification will be set up by such organizations as the Association for Advancement of Psychotherapy or the American Academy of Psychotherapists. Otherwise the public is at the mercy of inadequate and untrained therapists, who at times do not hesitate to tackle very complex and difficult problems with harmful results. Enough knowledge of psychotherapy has already been accumulated to make it a definitive discipline that can be learned in an orderly and organized fashion, with graduation as the reward and consequently a much greater protection for patients.

16

Psychotherapy and Western Philosophical Tradition

This chapter provides a conclusion to the technical discussion of how psychotherapy heals by offering the reader some perspective on the concept of psychotherapy as based on Western philosophical tradition. The subject has been treated exhaustively by Bromberg (1954) and the purpose here is only to remind the reader of certain essential points of orientation in Western philosophical thought that form the basis for all modern psychotherapeutic endeavor.

To illustrate the orientation of Western philosophy that was conducive to the development of psychotherapeutic techniques, we shall discuss Plato, Aristotle, and Spinoza.

The Greek skeptical spirit is best illustrated by the Socratic method of philosophical dialogue; as such it is properly called the "Socratic spirit." The origins of this method are described in Plato's *Phaedo.** It is called the method of *dialectic* (which properly means "conversation") and proceeds on the idea that truth has to be reached or approached by a debate between two inquirers or within the heart of a single inquirer, as his "soul" questions itself

* It should be noted that Plato, in contrast to Socrates, was not a humanist. Thus we speak of the "Socratic spirit," not the "Platonic spirit."

and answers its own questions. Hypotheses are formed and the consequences of the hypotheses are deduced and examined. As greater numbers of such consequences are shown to be the case, so our belief in the truth of the hypotheses is enhanced. As Taylor (1953) points out:

> The method ascribed to Socrates in the *Phaedo* is clearly in principle that which has proved itself the one path to truth in scientific theory down to our own time.

There is plenty of Socratic investigation going on today in the realm of logic and metamathematics, but there has been a tendency to forget that Socrates primarily emphasized and focused his investigation on individual human problems of living.

Granted that hypotheses about human living cannot be proved with such accuracy as those in mathematics, this does not make the investigation of human living hopeless or justify withdrawal into symbolic logic. It merely indicates that our conclusions must be tentative and subject to continuous reexamination as long as we live.

Socrates believed that the study of philosophy was the *same discipline* as the study of human living, and that through the method of dialectic we could even obtain knowledge of ethical principles as well as values and guidelines on how to live.

This problem is taken up in great detail in Plato's *Protagoras*, where a number of important principles are discussed. Socrates tries to demonstrate to the cynical Sophist—who believes that since man is the measure of all things, therefore the whole idea of values is chimerical—that *virtue and knowledge have a very intimate relationship.* The good life will be found by the man with the most knowledge, proposes Socrates, and this is the central thesis of his philosophy.

Although it is debatable, one might argue that in the same dialogue Socrates also establishes a rudimentary pleasure-pain principle of behavior. He pictures man attempting by the use of reason to gain the greatest possible amount of pleasure and to avoid as much pain as he can. We see Socrates conceiving of the rational man using all the knowledge and the reason at his disposal in an attempt to achieve the best possible life. This makes Plato the first "psychologically minded" philosopher; his ideal is man acting on principles gained through a dialectical process of self-enlightenment.

The "psychological-mindedness" of a philosopher (or any individual) is a necessary prerequisite to the employment of dialectical investigation in a philosophy focused on the good life. It consists of the inherent capacity to understand and examine human behavior in terms of its deeper motivations rather than to be befuddled and lulled by the usual rationalizations and defenses. It involves a certain ability to follow the emotional logic of behavior, in a sense analogous to the ability of the physicist to grasp the mathematical organization of field problems.

Plato in a number of other instances indicates considerable insight into human psychology. For example, in *The Republic* he discusses the nature of dreams. "Bestial" desires in the state of sleep are able to express themselves; he explains this as due to the "gentle" parts of the soul in the state of sleep being somewhat weakened and therefore not as well able to control and conceal these "bestial" features.

In other dialogues including the *Gorgias,* Plato discusses quite at length the most original and significant contribution of his thought, the notion of the soul. The soul possesses intellectual consciousness, is the seat of knowledge and error, and is responsible for man's thought and actions. In this primitive notion of the personality, given rather consistently within Plato's philosophy, there are conceived to be in the soul a number of conflicting desires or aims that he sometimes groups in the "bestial" and the "gentler" categories.

For Plato the common principle of epistemology and ethics is to "make the soul as good as possible." As Taylor (1953) explains, this for Plato would be the supreme business of man:

> . . . on the one side to attain the knowledge of existence as it really is, on the other to base one's moral conduct on a true knowledge of "moral values." . . . As science is ruined by the confusion of fancy with fact, so practical life is spoiled by a false estimate of the good.

Plato recognized that one of the important ways of attaining happiness is for man by the use of reason to govern the parts of his soul so as to facilitate the functioning of the whole being toward the morally permissible attainment of the maximum amount of the highest pleasures. He establishes a hierarchy of pleasures and shows how knowledge of this will enable a man to direct his aims at the best or deepest of pleasurable activities while maintaining an internal and external harmony.

A similar tradition assuming the importance of connecting the study of philosophy and the study of human living was followed by Aristotle. Aristotle is not as dramatic as Socrates in his emphasis on the intimate relationship between knowledge and the good life; nevertheless, he more formally considers the relationship between the mind, the body, and the good life.

Aristotle proposes in *De Anima* that mind and body are aspects of a single substance, standing to one another in the relation of form to matter. There is, moreover, no sharp dividing line between the functions of life, such as breathing, digestion, and sleep, and the conscious mental processes. It follows, therefore, that the human species is not so different from other species. We are distinguished only insofar as our exercise of the lower powers is modified to a greater degree by the presence of reason. For a detailed discussion of Aristotle's formal views on these matters, which is outside the scope of this text, see the excellent books by D. J. Allen (1952) and W. D. Ross (1959).

Aristotle held that the general name for the motive force to which animals are subject is *desire (orexis)* and this may present itself in three forms—desire for something conceived as the good, anger, and desire for pleasure. The first of these—desire for something conceived as the good—differs from the other two forms of desire in having an object that is not a particular, and is evidently limited to rational beings who have a sense of time and the power of generalization.

It follows from this that the difference between ourselves and animals is not that they are creatures of pure impulse, whereas we are subject to a blend of impulse and reason, but that they are guided by a sporadic imagination of things pleasant and painful, whereas man *also* can have, if he wishes, a rational conception of the good. Man, by the use of reason, can arrive at goals of living that he thinks are valuable. In a man a "bestial" desire may conflict with his conception of the good and give rise to excruciating mental tensions.

Aristotle in the *Ethics* proposes a solution aimed at preventing these forms of tension from arising. As with Plato, his solution suffers from lack of insight into unconscious forces, but still he proposes rules for reaching the good life. The problem, writes Aristotle, is to bring practical reason into a permanent alliance with the desire for what our rational conception is of the truly good. We should try to possess both the true conception of the good at which we ought to aim, and sufficient impetus and means of acting in the right direction so as to be able to resist momentary attractions.

Aristotle therefore puts maximum emphasis on the importance of philosophy to human everyday life. First, it is important in developing a rational conception of what is truly good. He considers philosophy important also in that the contemplative life is the best life; philosophy is best because we do not seek philosophy for the sake of any other advantage, but rather "we pursue this as the only free science, and it alone exists for its own sake." This is really an extension of the Socratic conception of philosophy being based on human wonder and thought, the most characteristic function of man; in the exercise of philosophy he most realizes his potential.

At times in the *Ethics*, Aristotle was trying to establish a way of life for the individual, arrived at by active philosophizing. This is the classical Socratic concept of living, formulated in an age in which the development of the free and enlightened man was considered to be the most important accomplishment of the human race. This spirit emphasizes the development of the free and enlightened man, who sets the goals of his own life through the use of his reason.

Although it contains some internal contradictions, Aristotle's ethical study has the primary aim of promoting and maintaining individual human happiness. The happiness or the highest good is variously conceived by the different classes of men but, Aristotle argues, it is easy to see that it must consist not only of idleness or sensuous enjoyment, which is guided by sporadic imagination of things pleasant and painful and thus often accompanied by unhappiness, but in rational or contemplative activity. This is an extension of Plato's argument of the importance of reason in helping man discover the method by which the most pleasure is to be found. Man is partly emotional and sensitive and partly a rational being, and the happiness of the creature thus constituted will consist in two forms of rational activity, according to Aristotle. These are the free exercise of reason, and the discipline of the emotions, according to rules or purposes formulated by reason.

Aristotle pictures the happiest life as being one in which man, by the free exercise of reason, decides on certain modes of behavior, and then disciplines his emotions and "bestial" desires according to these conclusions. He also mentions the great importance of the early establishment of *good habits*, or habits of virtuous activity, to the later development of the individual.

In summary, the Greek philosophers offer certain basic principles that form the intellectual starting point for all psychotherapy. Their key tenets are:

1. The study of philosophy should have principal focus on the study of human living, or, as Aristotle states, "the act proper to intellect is life."

2. Through knowledge of self and the world one can discover the values and behavior patterns that will lead to a good life and concomitantly to happiness. Correlated with this is the importance of the development of good habits early in life, which may later be used for the purposes of guiding behavior toward those

values that human reason decides to be uppermost. There is a fascinating suggestion here of the religion of Confucius, with its stress on the close connection of proper ritual conduct and happiness.

3. Problems of knowledge and epistemology are prior to, but inextricably bound up with, problems of human living.

4. Ethics should be primarily concerned with self-enlightenment and should be centered on the individual and his behavior. Such a concept is the fundamental starting point both to the Socratic spirit and to dynamic psychiatry, although the latter has developed a much more profound understanding of the problem.

There is one more extremely important "psychologically minded" philosopher who deserves special mention in our discussion of the Western philosophical tradition as the basis of psychotherapy. This philosopher is Spinoza, a man for whom philosophy was inextricably bound up with human behavior, and a noble man who lived by his own conclusions. As Russell (1945) states, "ethically he is supreme," and Russell admires Spinoza's capacity to live nobly, even recognizing the great limitations of human power.

Spinoza believed that the universe consisted of an indivisible "unity of Substance" containing an infinite number of attributes. Only two of these are known to man, *Cogitatio* or thought and *Extensio* or extension. Everything is ruled by an absolute logical necessity in this Parmenidean system. Thus the individual man is subordinated to the order of nature, and is merely a configuration of attributes. His philosophy leads to the denial of personal immortality, and to highly deterministic ethics; for these unorthodox ideas Spinoza was very much persecuted.

We cannot accept Spinoza's metaphysical views today, but this still does not detract from his spirit of inquiry and focus on human living. Significantly, his major work, *Ethics*, consists of three parts: metaphysics, psychology, and finally an ethic based on the first two subjects. Of special interest to us is Part IV: "On Human Servitude or the Strength of the Emotions."

Spinoza is paradoxical in that he does allow for a certain amount of human freedom. He would characterize this as the power of the mind to gain by reason (dialectical investigation or self-enlightenment) a clearer understanding of things. *In so doing one approaches happiness,* a principle based on the Socratic spirit.

If we go along with Spinoza, we are faced with a paradoxical situation. On the one hand Spinoza is trying on metaphysical grounds to maintain a highly deterministic ethics. On the other hand, he is praising individuality and the development of personal essence as essential to happiness.

Part of the problem is solved by not accepting Spinoza's metaphysics, but this does not negate Spinoza's insight into the true nature of human bondage:

> A man who is submissive to his emotions is not in power over himself, but in the hands of fortune to such an extent that he is often constrained although he may see what is better for him to follow what is worse.

Dynamic psychiatry believes that man can gain increasing happiness as he is relieved of servitude toward the emotions, a servitude engendered in unconscious mental conflicts. However, we increasingly stress the importance of the individual essence of a man, while retaining the deterministic view that human activity is to a great extent dependent on unconscious processes for motivation.

We still retain Spinoza's conception of man being unhappy and agitated by external causes insofar as he is in servitude to emotional conflicts, and becoming free and happy by the process of deriving a clearer understanding of things both internal and external. Thus in Spinoza's terms a man's happiness consists of being able to preserve his own essence. Hesse (1968) puts the problem in a more modern context at the start of his revolutionary novel *Demian,* so popular with today's youth:

> I wanted only to try to live in accord with the promptings
> which came from my true self. Why was that so very difficult?

Following the philosophical notions presented here we could say that the rational or cultured man by the process of dialectical investigation achieves self-enlightenment, knows himself and the world, and studies the best of what has been thought and said in the world. On the basis of this he develops a theory of values, a right conception of the ends of life, increased freedom from emotional conflict, and a higher realization of his own human potential or "essence," thereby approaching happiness.

Psychotherapy, on an intellectual level, represents the logical extension of this process. When something has gone wrong on the road to emotional maturity and the individual is so in the grips of psychopathology that a reasonable and fruitful approach to life cannot be followed, it is time for psychotherapy. As Russell (1945) puts it, Aristotle's *Ethics* are of little use to a man "possessed by the devil," in the grip of emotional agitations of all sorts.

It is reasonable to conclude from the preceding discussion that the intellectual basis of psychotherapy is provided by and is consistent with the Western philosophical tradition. However, in the process of psychotherapy itself, matters become much more extremely complicated. In fact, as one moves from rational philosophy, on the one hand, through counseling and supportive therapy, and finally to intensive long-term psychotherapy, on the other hand, the role of the unconscious in the process begins to take great precedence over intellectual aspects.

One of the pitfalls of attempting intensive long-term psychotherapy lies in underestimating the emotional aspects, the role of the unconscious mental life, and the transference, thus attempting to view it as an intellectual process. This is an amateur blunder that can lead to the most damaging explosions, entirely unexpected by the therapist, or to the most tangled emotional involvements and counterinvolvements that may threaten serious harm to both patient and therapist.

It has been the purpose of this book to give the reader an

overview of the various complicated aspects of intensive long-term psychotherapy. I have attempted to explore the various nonrational aspects of psychotherapy in the greatest possible detail to illustrate both the complexity and the emotional depth of the process.

One oversimplifies this process called "psychotherapy" at one's own peril. Over the past fifty years a number of rather narcissistic individuals have set up "schools" of psychotherapy that emphasize one aspect or another of the process as we have described it. This is both poor science and poor philosophy in our age of field theory and quantum mechanics.

I fervently hope that greater interdisciplinary cooperation in the study of psychotherapy can be achieved from the various fields of behavioral sciences, and that philosophers can be interested in the many challenging aspects of the subject and encouraged to work with scientists and psychotherapists toward the common goal of helping psychotherapy heal.

17

Summary and Conclusions

Presented here for the purposes of review and reiteration are the principal arguments and contributions of the book, in summary form.

Chapter 1: Professional persons learning or doing long-term intensive psychotherapy often do not have a sufficient grasp of the complex nature of the process. Training programs tend to be insufficient in their attention to the substantial body of knowledge already accumulated about the process of psychotherapy, leaving the public in danger of psychotherapists who tend to "drift" into long-term intensive psychotherapy with patients, without the proper knowledge and training. This book attempts to focus on certain aspects of this process that have been somewhat glossed over in other texts.

Chapter 2: When we speak of curative processes in psychotherapy, we do not address ourselves to the cure of any specific "diseases," since in psychiatry there are no specific "diseases" but only preponderant reaction patterns or clusters of symptoms. These in turn are manifestations of emotional immaturity, defined essentially as being based on unhealthy development of ego functions and leading to a disorder of relationships among the functioning parts of the personality and consequently to difficulties between the individual and other people. The roots of all unhealthy ego functions are found in the mother-child symbiosis in the earliest years of life, although later childhood relationships with parents and siblings can also substantially affect the "childhood nucleus" that forms in all human beings. The healing process of psychotherapy must address itself to this childhood core of our personalities, or there is no fundamental change.

Chapter 3: The definition of psychoanalytically oriented psychotherapy is outlined, and three important debates about what constitutes such therapy are reviewed. Discussion of these debates leads to the conclusion that every psychotherapy ideally should be predominantly investigative in procedure at the beginning. If it appears that the patient cannot tolerate such investigation, or if after about six months it is apparent that he utilizes the investigation only for gratification, goals should be modified and a simple supportive psychotherapy should be considered. If the investigative procedure is tolerated, then either a full-blown transference neurosis will develop or only relatively minor manifestations of transference will appear. In the former situation we have the conditions for a psychoanalysis, with resolution of the transference neurosis through interpretation and consequent insight; in the latter situation we have a psychoanalytically oriented psychotherapy dealing mainly with derivatives of infantile conflicts.

The advantage of this approach is that it tailors the therapy to the needs and limitations of the patient and enables each patient to "go as far as he can go" within these needs and limitations, rather than forcing the patient into some preconceived notions of what therapy he should have.

Chapter 4: The concept of "supportive therapy" is reviewed, and doubt is cast on the efficacy of manipulation of the environment as a supportive therapeutic measure. In stressful situations during all forms of psychotherapy the therapist from time to time must resort to supportive measures, and, if well timed, this can have an important and powerful impact on the patient.

Chapter 5: The terms "transference," "transference neurosis," and "transference psychosis" are defined. A transference neurosis can occur in psychoanalytically oriented psychotherapy, and is not to be feared if it develops spontaneously. Beginners tend to try to break this up by either stopping the treatment or attempting to gratify directly the intense needs expressed. The former procedure is experienced by the patient as a crushing rejection; the latter procedure tends to fix the patient on the supposed omnipotence of the therapist. When a therapeutically workable transference neurosis appears, we may change the definition of what we are doing from "psychoanalytically oriented psychotherapy" to "psychoanalysis," regardless of the frequency of the sessions or whether a couch is being used, but this is a matter of semantics.

The term "transference-resistance" is sometimes used to indicate the appearance of transference manifestations when repressed material is about to emerge, thus changing the focus of the therapy away from this material. Or it can be termed "transference-resistance" when the therapy is stalemated either by a psychotic denial with the patient insisting that obvious transference manifestations are not transference, or by fixation by the patient on getting gratification in the transference rather than any interest in the investigative process.

Gratification in the transference can be useful in situations where anxiety becomes intolerable. The skillful therapist, both by good timing of interpretations and by knowing when to allow some gratification in the transference, keeps anxiety at an optimal level for therapeutic progress.

Chapter 6: Interpretations must be based on a clear understanding of unconscious material. Properly timed interpretations should lead to insight, and the difference between intellectual and emotional insight is discussed. Dream interpretation can be utilized in psychoanalytically oriented psychotherapy, provided that careful selection is made of the material in order to relate the dream to the focus and level of what is being discussed. Inexact interpretations, if properly used, represent a supportive measure and provide intellectual defenses; if used improperly they lead to fixed resistances.

Chapter 7: The concept of "working through" is defined as a basically intellectual process consisting of three major operational processes. These are the fitting of the patient's descriptions of events to those of the therapist, repeated interpretation characterized by a waxing and waning of anxiety as the manifold forms and connections of the unconscious are revealed, and a subtle conditioning procedure that influences the thought and behavior of the patient in a direction the therapist wants him to go. Working through is arbitrarily differentiated from "after-education" for purposes of presentation. The latter is conceived as a more general set of emotional processes that go on between patient and therapist, and is discussed in Chapter 9. The need for working through is proved by the lag period during which newly acquired perceptions and attitudes must be translated into more healthy patterns of behavior.

Chapter 8: The required conditions for an optimal working alliance in psychotherapy to be formed and maintained are the inhibition of "acting-out" and "acting-in" on the part of both therapist and patient, a therapeutic atmosphere, an ego in the patient capable of certain key functions, and continual scrutiny of the therapeutic alliance through a mutual exploration of the state of the alliance.

The terms "countertransference," "countertransference structure," and "countertransference neurosis" are defined. The last of these is always undesirable. Countertransference can be utilized in achieving further understanding of the patient, and common ways that countertransference makes its appearance are listed. A particularly tricky aspect of countertransference is the element represented by an unconscious transference from the therapist to the patient. This leads to an examination of "after-education."

Chapter 9: Controversial definitions of "after-education" are discussed, in which this concept is viewed as ranging all the way from conscious role-playing by the therapist to an unconscious interaction between therapist and patient. The highly controversial subject of an unconscious symbiotic fusion between patient and therapist at certain stages of the therapy is raised, or, in other terms, the concept of incorporation of the therapist and its effect on the patient is discussed. Clinical experience indicates great variability from patient to patient and from therapist to therapist in this kind of experience. It is clear that it is a mistake to speak of psychotherapy as healing in only one way, and to insist that if that way is not followed—whether it be the interpretation of full-blown transference neurosis or an unconscious symbiosis with the therapist—healing will not take place. This underestimates the flexibility of patients and their capacity to find what they need from a decent therapist regardless of his theoretical orientation—sometimes in spite of it. It also underestimates the complexity and variety of potentials for healing in the therapeutic relationship.

Chapter 10: The conduct of the psychotherapist can vitally influence psychotherapy. His conduct, the way he lives his life, how he relates to people, and how he carries on his professional activities give a clear message to the patient, regardless of what he may express verbally. The presentation of conflicting messages—verbal vs. his conduct—can lead to a double-bind situation quite destructive to psychotherapy. Furthermore, his conduct can lead to serious interference with his capacity for empathy and can convert him from a humanist to a withdrawn and self-centered bureaucrat. The actual behavior of the therapist is the vital determinant for the development of trust in the patient. The handling of payment for psychotherapy is discussed as an example of how the conduct of the therapist is a mirror of his doctrines.

Chapter 11: This is the first chapter of a section of the book devoted to special problems of contemporary importance in psychotherapy. These days the psychotherapist frequently has to deal with what the patient presents as "existential anxiety," which often represents a displacement from pathological anxiety. If the sources of the pathological anxiety are ameliorated, this "existential anxiety" tends to disappear.

There are no compelling arguments to elevate the "anxiety of nonbeing" or "existential anxiety" to the status of neurotic or pathological anxiety as a motivating force in personality function. This remains a controversial philosophical concept, and the importance of it is not generally agreed upon.

It is not necessary either to abandon reason in order to overcome "existential anxiety" or to make any mysterious "leaps" into religious faith. Such a procedure is a matter of personal choice. The development of mature object-relations, the adoption of a Stoic philosophy, and the participation in the communal human experiences of art and beauty are also available.

The psychotherapist must be aware of this problem and be prepared to deal with "existential anxiety" as a displacement from neurotic anxiety; when this displacement is unraveled, it is up to the patient to solve any residue of "true existential anxiety."

Chapter 12: The borderline patient and the special problems he presents to the therapist illustrate the many important factors involved in psychotherapy as described in this book. The most common erroneous responses to these difficult patients are, first, attempts to minister directly to the patient's needs for "tender loving care" and, second, to adopt a too detached and analytic approach, hiding behind rigid rules of "technique." If one can successfully walk a tightrope between these two horns of the therapist's "crucial dilemma" in the treatment of borderline patients, after-education as we have discussed it can occur. The patient introjects the warm inner attitude of the therapist toward him, better ego-adaptative techniques, and a calm investigative atmosphere in which to examine himself.

All these provide the tools to make a gradual modification in the basic malevolent introjects and thereby catalyze a genuine change in the patient in the direction of cure. A variety of important factors thus work together in the complex process of healing the borderline patient through the medium of psychotherapy, and the mature therapist must be aware of and capable of dealing with all of these factors.

Chapter 13: A variety of different problems involved in didactic training in psychotherapy are reviewed. The three traditional didactic methods—individual supervision, case seminars, and individual or seminar-directed reading—all have serious problems and limitations. Their effectiveness remains poorly tested and their use based more on tradition and lack of better ideas than anything else. An annotated bibliography is presented as a guide for seminar leaders and students toward an orderly progression through the most valuable reading.

Chapter 14: The term "metapsychiatry" is introduced to

cover the investigation of the scientific and artistic aspects of psychotherapy and to locate psychotherapy in the Western philosophical tradition. Under Popper's conception of science as consisting of conjectures and refutations, and demarcated from philosophy by possessing the potential for crucial experimental refutation, psychotherapy lies on the border between scientific and philosophical knowledge. Although it has progressed like a science, proper crucial experiments have not been (and perhaps cannot be) devised to refute whole theoretical approaches in psychotherapy. However, a body of clinical experience and research knowledge (Strupp and Bergin 1969) has accumulated, which acts to refute conjectures about specific situations and places the psychotherapy process in detail toward the scientific category in Popper's sense. The delineation of scientific and artistic and philosophical aspects of psychotherapy and the careful separation of those aspects that can be studied by scientific method and those aspects that must appeal to "common experience of mankind" for verification remain the future tasks of metapsychiatry.

Chapter 15: The artistic factors in psychotherapy are restricted in this text to certain creative, intuitive, or empathic features in the person of the therapist that cannot be taught or even formalized. The psychotherapist is not an artist—he is caught between "the two cultures," a situation demanding considerable maturity and self-identity.

To be "in tune" with one's own unconscious or the unconscious of others depends partly on one's state of ego functioning and partly on certain innate capacities. Professional persons with the capacity to empathize with others and to enter into a feeling relationship with others at a deep level should be encouraged to obtain good training as psychotherapists. It is hoped that the American Board of Psychiatry will be modified to separate those truly qualified to do psychotherapy by virtue of ability and experience from those who are not. Furthermore, the Association for the Advancement of Psychotherapy and the American Academy of Psychotherapists are urged to develop ideal programs and certification of truly qualified individuals who intend to do psychotherapy.

Otherwise the public is at the mercy of inadequate and untrained therapists who unfortunately do not hesitate at times to tackle very complex and deep problems with harmful, sometimes lethal, results. Enough knowledge of psychotherapy has accumulated so that it can be systematically taught with graduation and certification as the reward for proficiency in the field. This affords the best protection for patients.

Chapter 16: It is reasonable to conclude, from the discussion in this chapter, that the intellectual basis of psychotherapy is provided by and is consistent with the Western philosophical tradition. However, in the process of psychotherapy, matters become much more extremely complicated. As one moves from philosophy, through counseling and supportive therapy to psychoanalytically oriented psychotherapy, the role of the unconscious in the process begins to take great precedence over intellectual aspects. It is a mark of the beginner to be unaware of this fact, and dangerous results can occur. This book has therefore concentrated on the nonrational aspects of psychotherapy.

The multiple aspects of the psychotherapy process invite cooperation by numerous disciplines such as psychiatry, psychology, sociology, and philosophy to promote better understanding of this extremely important subject. The greater our understanding of the various aspects of the psychotherapy process, the better our rate of effectiveness as psychotherapists can become. If this is combined with more careful training in the field, the entire general level of psychotherapy can be raised—an elevation of level that is at present badly needed.

BIBLIOGRAPHY

ADLER, M. (1965): *The Conditions of Philosophy.* New York: Atheneum Publishers.

AICHORN, A. (1945): *Wayward Youth.* New York: Viking Press.

ALEXANDER, F. (1956): *Psychoanalysis and Psychotherapy.* New York: W. W. Norton and Co.

———, and T. French. (1946): *Psychoanalytic Therapy.* New York: Ronald Press.

ALLEN, D. J. (1952): *Philosophy of Aristotle.* London: Oxford University Press.

ALTMAN, L. (1969): *The Dream in Psychoanalysis.* New York: International Universities Press.

ARIETI, S. (1955): *Interpretation of Schizophrenia.* New York: Brunner.

BEIER, E. (1966): *The Silent Language of Psychotherapy.* Chicago: Aldine.

BELLAK, L. (1958): *Schizophrenia.* New York: Logos Press.

BERNE, E. (1964): *Games People Play.* New York: Grove Press.

BLEULER, E. (1950): *Dementia Praecox or the Group of Schizophrenias.* New York: International Universities Press.

BLOS, P. (1962): *On Adolescence.* New York: Free Press of Glencoe.

BRADY, J. (1967): "Psychotherapy, Learning Theory and Insight," *Archives of General Psychiatry,* 16:304-311.

BRENNER, C. (1955): *An Elementary Textbook of Psychoanalysis.* New York: International Universities Press.

BRODY E., AND R. REDLICH (eds.). (1952): *Psychotherapy with Schizophrenics.* New York: International Universities Press.

BRODY, S., AND S. AXELRAD. (1966): "Anxiety, Socialization and Ego Formation in Infancy," *International Journal of Psycho-Analysis,* 47:-218-235.

BROMBERG, W. (1954): *Man Above Humanity.* Philadelphia: J. B. Lippincott.

———. (1962): *The Nature of Psychotherapy.* New York: Grune and Stratton.

BRUSTEIN, R. (1964): *The Theatre of Revolt.* Boston: Little, Brown and Co.

CAMUS, A. (1955): *The Myth of Sisyphus.* New York: Alfred A. Knopf.

———. (1957): *The Stranger.* New York: Alfred A. Knopf.

CHESSICK, R. D. (1961): "Some Problems and Pseudo-Problems in Psychiatry," *Psychiatric Quarterly,* 35:711-719.

———. (1965): "Empathy and Love in Psychotherapy," *American Journal of Psychotherapy,* 19:205-219.

———. (1966): "Office Psychotherapy of Borderland Patients," *American Journal of Psychotherapy,* 20:600-614.

———. (1967a): "Greed and Vanity in the Life of the Psychotherapist," *Psychiatry Digest,* 28:40-43.

———. (1967b): "Anxiety and Maternal Love," *American Journal of Psychotherapy,* 21:325-327.

———. (1967c): "Ethical and Psychodynamic Aspects of Payment for Psychotherapy," *Voices,* 3:26-30.

———. (1968): "The 'Crucial Dilemma' of the Therapist in the Psychotherapy of Borderland Patients," *American Journal of Psychotherapy,* 22:655-666.

———. (May 1969; to be published): "The Prediction Seminar for Teaching Psychotherapy," presented at meeting of the American Psychiatric Association.

———, and R. McFarland. (1963): "Problems in Psychopharmacological Research," *Journal of the American Medical Association,* 185:237-241.

CHESSICK, R. D., *et al.* (1966a): "The Effect of Morphine, Chlorpromazine, Pentobarbital and Placebo on 'anxiety,' " *Journal of Nervous and Mental Disease,* 141:540-548.

———. (1966b): "A Comparison of the Effect of Infused Catecholemines and Certain Affect States," *American Journal of Psychiatry,* 123:156-165.

COHEN, M. B. (1952): "Countertransference and Anxiety," *Psychiatry,* 15:231-243.

COLBY, K. (1951): *A Primer for Psychotherapists.* New York: Ronald Press.

DEUTSCH, H. (1965): *Neuroses and Character Types.* New York: International Universities Press.

DEWALD, P. (1964): *Psychotherapy.* New York: Basic Books.

EISSLER, K. (1952): "Remarks on the Psychoanalysis of Schizophrenia," in E. Brody and F. Redlich (eds.), *Psychotherapy with Schizophrenics*. New York: International Universities Press.

EKSTEIN, R., AND R. WALLERSTEIN. (1958): *The Teaching and Learning of Psychotherapy*. New York: Basic Books.

ENGLISH, O., AND S. FINCH. (1957): *Introduction to Psychiatry*. New York: W. W. Norton and Co.

ENGLISH, O., AND G. PEARSON. (1963): *Emotional Problems of Living*. New York: W. W. Norton and Co.

ERIKSON, E. (1950): *Childhood and Society*. New York: W. W. Norton and Co.

FENICHEL, O. (1941): "Problems of Psychoanalytic Technique," *Psychoanalytic Quarterly*.

————. (1945): *Psychoanalytic Theory of the Neuroses*. New York: W. W. Norton and Co.

FERENCZI, S. (1926): "The Further Development of an Active Therapy in Psychoanalysis," in *Further Contributions*. London: Hogarth Press.

FLEMING, J., AND T. BENEDEK. "Supervision," *Psychoanalytic Quarterly*, 33:71-96.

FLIESS, R. (1948): *The Psychoanalytic Reader*. New York: International Universities Press.

FORD, E. "Being and Becoming a Psychotherapist: The Search for Identity," *American Journal of Psychotherapy*, 17:472-482.

FRANK, J. (1961): *Persuasion and Healing*. Baltimore: Johns Hopkins Press.

————. (1968): "The Role of Hope in Psychotherapy," *International Journal of Psychiatry*, 5:383-412.

FRENCH, T., AND E. FROMM. (1964): *Dream Interpretation*. New York: Basic Books.

FREUD, A. (1946): *The Ego and the Mechanisms of Defense*. New York: International Universities Press.

FREUD, S. (1958): *Recommendations to Physicians Practicing Psycho-Analysis* (1912). Standard Edition, Vol. XII. London: Hogarth Press.

————. (1958): *Observations on Transference Love* (1913). Standard Edition, Volume XII. London: Hogarth Press.

————. (1958): *On Beginning the Treatment* (1913). Standard Edition, Volume XII. London: Hogarth Press.

————. (1958): *Remembering, Repeating and Working Through* (1913). Standard Edition, Volume XII. London: Hogarth Press.

————. (1957): *On the History of the Psychoanalytic Movement* (1914). Standard Edition, Volume XIV. London: Hogarth Press.

————. (1963): *Introductory Lectures on Psychoanalysis* (1915, 1916). Standard Edition, Volumes XV and XVI. London: Hogarth Press.

————. (1957): *Some Character Types Met with in Psychoanalytic Work* (1916). Standard Edition, Volume XIV. London: Hogarth Press.

————. (1961): *The Ego and the Id* (1923). Standard Edition, Volume XIX. London: Hogarth Press.

————. (1959): *Inhibitions, Symptoms and Anxiety* (1926). Standard Edition, Volume XX. London: Hogarth Press.

————. (1961): *The Future of an Illusion* (1927). Standard Edition, Volume XXI. London: Hogarth Press.

————. (1961): *Civilization and Its Discontents* (1930). Standard Edition, Volume XXI. London: Hogarth Press.

————. (1964): *An Outline of Psychoanalysis* (1938). Standard Edition, Volume XXIII. London: Hogarth Press.

FRIEDMANN, M. (1955): *Martin Buber: The Life of Dialogue.* Chicago: University of Chicago Press.

FROMM, E. (1955): *The Sane Society.* New York: Rinehart and Co.

————. (1956, 1963): *The Art of Loving.* New York: Bantam Books.

FROMM-REICHMANN, F. (1950): *Principles of Intensive Psychotherapy.* Chicago: University of Chicago Press.

————. (1959): *Psychoanalysis and Psychotherapy.* Chicago: University of Chicago Press.

GALBRAITH, J. K. (1958): *The Affluent Society.* New York: Mentor Books.

GEDO, J. (1964): "Concepts for Classification of the Psychotherapies," *International Journal of Psycho-Analysis,* 45:530-539.

GIOVACCHINI, P. (1965): "Transference, Incorporation and Synthesis," *International Journal of Psycho-Analysis,* 46:287-396.

————. (1967): "The Frozen Introject," *International Journal of Psycho-Analysis,* 48:61-67.

————, with B. BOYER. (1967a): *Psychoanalytic Treatment of Characterological and Schizophrenic Disorders.* New York: Science House.

GITELSON, M. (1952): "Emotional Problems of the Analyst in the Psychoanalytic Situation," *International Journal of Psycho-Analysis,* 35:1-10.

————. (1967): "Analytic Aphorisms," *Psychoanalytic Quarterly,* 36: 260-270.

GLOVER, E. (1955): *The Techniques of Psychoanalysis.* New York: International Universities Press.

GREENSON, R. (1965): "The Working Alliance and the Transference Neurosis," *Psychoanalytic Quarterly,* 34:155-181.

————. (1968): *The Technique and Practice of Psychoanalysis.* New York: International Universities Press.

————, AND M. WEXLER. (1969): "The Nontransference Relationship in the Psychoanalytic Situation," *International Journal of Psycho-Analysis,* 50:27-40.

GRINKER, R. R. (1965): "Identity or Regression in American Pychoanalysis," *Archives of General Psychiatry*, 12:113-125.

————, *et al.* (1968): *The Borderline Syndrome*. New York: Basic Books.

GUIORA, A., *et al.* (1967): "The Continuous Case Seminar," *Psychiatry*, 30:44-59.

GUNTRIP, H. (1968): *Schizoid Phenomena, Object Relations and The Self.* New York: International Universities Press.

HALMOS, P. L. (1966): *The Faith of the Counsellors*. New York: Schocken Books.

HARRISON, S., AND D. CAREK. (1966): *A Guide to Psychotherapy*. Boston: Little, Brown and Co.

HEIMANN, P. (1950): "On Countertransference," *International Journal of Psycho-Analysis*, 31:81-84.

HESSE, H. (1968): *Demian*. New York: Bantam Books.

HILL, L. B. (1955): *Psychotherapeutic Intervention in Schizophrenia*. Chicago: University of Chicago Press.

HOLLENDER, M. (1965): *The Practice of Psychoanalytic Psychotherapy*. New York: Grune and Stratton.

HOLLINGSHEAD, A., AND F. REDLICH. (1958): *Social Class and Mental Illness*. New York: John Wiley and Sons.

HUXLEY, A. (1963): *Literature and Science*. New York: Harper and Row.

JASPERS, K. (1957): *The Great Philosophers*. New York: Harcourt, Brace and Co.

JONES, E. (1963): *The Life and Work of Sigmund Freud*. New York: Anchor Books.

JONES, W. (1952): *A History of Western Philosophy*. New York: Harcourt, Brace and Co.

JUNG, C. (1933): *Modern Man in Search of a Soul*. New York: Harcourt, Brace and Co.

KARUSH, A. (1967): "Working Through," *Psychoanalytic Quarterly*, 36: 497-531.

KATZ, R. L. (1963): *Empathy, Its Nature and Uses*. New York: Free Press of Glencoe.

KAUFMANN, W. (1960): *From Shakespeare to Existentialism*. Garden City, N.Y.: Anchor Books.

KAZAN, E. (1967): *The Arrangement*. New York: Stein and Day.

KERNBERG, O. (1967): "Borderline Personality Organization," *Journal of the American Psychoanalytic Association*, 15:641.

————. (1968): "The Treatment of Patients with Borderline Personality Organization," *International Journal of Psycho-Analysis*, 49:600-619.

KIERKEGAARD, S. (1946): *The Concept of Dread*. Princeton, N.J.: Princeton University Press.

KNAPP, P., *et al.* (1966): "Asthma, Melancholia and Death," *Psychosomatic Medicine*, 28:114-133.

KNIGHT, R. P. (1954): *Psychoanalytic Psychiatry and Psychology.* New York: International Universities Press.

KOHUT, H. (1959): "Introspection, Empathy and Psychoanalysis," *Journal of the American Psychoanalytic Association,* 7:459.

KUHN, T. (1962): *Structure of Scientific Revolutions.* Chicago: University of Chicago Press.

LEVI, A. (1959): *Philosophy and the Modern World.* Bloomington, Ind.: Indiana University Press.

LIDZ, T. (1968): *The Person.* New York: Basic Books.

LIPSCHUTZ, D. (1955): "Transference in Borderline Cases," *Psychoanalytic Review,* 42:195.

LITOWITZ, N., AND K. NEWMAN. (1967): "Borderline Personality and the Theatre of the Absurd," *Archives of General Psychiatry,* 16:268.

LITTLE, M. (1966): "Transference in Borderline Cases," *International Journal of Psycho-Analysis,* 47:476.

McNEILL, W. (1963): *The Rise of the West.* Chicago: University of Chicago Press.

MARMOR, J. (1964): "Psychoanalytic Therapy and Theories of Learning," in J. H. Masserman (ed.), *Science and Psychoanalysis,* Volume VII, *Development and Research.* New York: Grune and Stratton, pp. 265-279.

————. (1966): "The Nature of the Psychotherapeutic Process," in O. Usdin (ed.), *Psychoneurosis and Schizophrenia.* Philadelphia: J. B. Lippincott.

MASSERMAN, J. H. (1955): *Practice of Dynamic Psychiatry.* Philadelphia: W. B. Saunders.

————. (1961): *Principles of Dynamic Psychiatry.* Philadelphia: W. B. Saunders.

MAZLISH, B. (1968): "Freud and Nietzsche," *Psychoanalytic Review,* 55:-360-375.

MENDELSON, M. (1960): *Psychoanalytic Concepts of Depression.* Springfield, Ill.: Charles C. Thomas.

MENNINGER, K. (1958): *Theory of Psychoanalytic Technique.* New York: Basic Books.

MODELL, A. (1968): *Object Love and Reality.* New York: International Universities Press.

MULLAHY, P. (1948): *Oedipus, Myth and Complex.* New York: Hermitage Press.

MUNROE, R. (1955): *Schools of Psychoanalytic Thought.* New York: Dryden Press.

NACHT, S. (1962): "Curative Factors in Psychoanalysis," *International Journal of Psycho-Analysis,* 43:206-211.

————. (1963): "The Non-Verbal Relationship in Psychoanalytic Treatment," *International Journal of Psycho-Analysis*, 44:328-333.

NIETZSCHE, F. (1969): *The Philosophy of Nietzsche.* New York: Random House.

NOVEY, S. (1962): "The Principle of 'Working Through' in Psychoanalysis," *Journal of the American Psychoanalytic Association*, 10:658-676.

NOYES, A., AND L. KOLB. (1963): *Modern Clinical Psychiatry.* Philadelphia: W. B. Saunders.

OATES, W. (ed.). (1940): *The Stoic and Epicurean Philosophers.* New York: Random House.

ODIER, C. (1956): *Anxiety and Magic Thinking.* New York: International Universities Press.

OLMSTED, J., AND E. OLMSTED. (1961): *Claude Bernard and the Experimental Method in Medicine.* New York: Collier Books.

ORNSTEIN, P. (1968): "Sorcerer's Apprentice: The Initial Phase of Training and Education in Psychiatry," *Comprehensive Psychiatry*, 9:293-315.

ORR, D. (1954): "Transference and Counter Transference: A Historical Survey," *Journal of the American Psychoanalytic Association*, 2:621-670.

PACHTER, H. (1961): *Paracelsus: Magic into Science.* New York: Collier Books.

POPPER, K. (1965): *Conjectures and Refutations.* New York: Basic Books.

RACKER, H. (1953): "Contribution to the Problem of Countertransference," *International Journal of Psycho-Analysis*, 34:313-324.

RADO, S., *et al.* (1963): Editorial, in *Archives of General Psychiatry*, 8:-527-529.

RAPAPORT, E. (1956): "The Management of an Eroticized Transference," *Psychoanlytic Quarterly*, 25:5.

REDLICH, F., AND D. FREEDMAN. (1967): *Theory and Practice of Psychiatry.* New York: Basic Books.

REICH, A. (1951): "On Countertransference," *International Journal of Psycho-Analysis*, 32:25-31.

REICH, W. (1949): *Character Analysis.* New York: Orgone Institute Press.

RHEINGOLD, J. (1967): *The Mother, Anxiety, and Death.* Boston: Little, Brown and Co.

ROAZEN, P. (1968): *Freud: Political and Social Thought.* New York: Alfred A. Knopf.

ROSS, W. D. (1959): *Aristotle.* New York: Meridian Books.

RUESCH, J. (1961): *Therapeutic Communication.* New York: W. W. Norton and Co.

RUSSELL, B. (1951): *The Conquest of Happiness* (1930). New York: Signet Books.

———. (1945): *History of Western Philosophy.* New York: Simon and Schuster.

————. (1959): *Wisdom of the West.* New York: Doubleday.

SANTAYANA, G. (1955): *Scepticism and Animal Faith.* New York: Dover Publications.

SARGANT, W. (1957): *Battle for the Mind.* New York: Doubleday.

SARTRE, J. (1964): *Nausea.* New York: New Directions.

SAUL, L. (1958): *Technic and Practice of Psychoanalysis.* Philadelphia: J. B. Lippincott.

————. (1960): *Emotional Maturity.* Philadelphia: J. B. Lippincott.

————. (1966): "The Concept of Emotional Maturity," *International Journal of Psychiatry,* 2:446-469.

SCHACHTEL, E. G. (1949): "On Memory and Childhood Amnesia," in P. Mullahy (ed.), *A Study of Interpersonal Relations.* New York: Grove Press.

SCHAFER, R. (1968): *Aspects of Internalization.* New York: International Universities Press.

SCHOFIELD, W. (1964): *Psychotherapy: The Purchase of Friendship.* Englewood Cliffs, N.J.: Prentice-Hall.

SCHWARTZ, E., AND T. ABEL. (1955): "The Professional Education of the Psychoanalytic Psychotherapist," *American Journal of Psychotherapy,* 9:253-261.

SEARLES, H. (1965): *Collected Papers.* New York: International Universities Press.

SECHEHAYE, M. (1951): *Symbolic Realization.* New York: International Universities Press.

SHANDS, H. (1960): *Thinking and Psychotherapy.* Cambridge, Mass.: Harvard University Press.

SHARAF, M., AND D. LEVINSON. (1964): "The Quest for Omnipotence in Professional Training," *Psychiatry,* 27:135-149.

SNOW, C. P. (1963): *The Two Cultures.* New York: Mentor Books.

STEWART, W. (1963): "An Inquiry into the Concept of Working Through," *Journal of the American Psychoanalytic Association,* 11:474-499.

STONE, L. (1961): *The Psychoanalytic Situation.* New York: International Universities Press.

STRUPP, H., AND A. BERGIN. (1969): "Some Empirical and Conceptual Bases for Coordinated Research in Psychotherapy," *International Journal of Psychiatry,* 7:18-90.

SULLIVAN, H. S. (1947): *Conceptions of Modern Psychiatry.* Washington, D.C.: W. A. White Foundation.

————. (1953): *The Interpersonal Theory of Psychiatry.* New York: W. W. Norton and Co.

————. (1956): *Clinical Studies in Psychiatry.* New York: W. W. Norton and Co.

————. (1962): *Schizophrenia as a Human Process.* New York: W. W. Norton and Co.

TARACHOW, S. (1963): *Introduction to Psychotherapy.* New York: International Universities Press.

TAYLOR, A. E. (1953): *Socrates.* New York: Anchor Books.

TILLICH, P. L. (1952): *The Courage To Be.* New Haven, Conn.: Yale University Press.

TISCHLER, G. L. (1968): "The Beginning Resident and Supervision," *Archives of Psychiatry,* 19:418-422.

TORREY, N. (1968): *The Spirit of Voltaire.* New York: Russell and Russell.

TOWER, L. (1956): "Countertransference," *Journal of the American Psychoanalytic Association,* 4:224-255.

UNAMUNO, M. (1954): *Tragic Sense of Life.* New York: Dover Publications.

VEITH, I. (1965): *Hysteria: The History of a Disease.* Chicago: University of Chicago Press.

WAELDER, R. (1960): *Basic Theory of Psychoanalysis.* New York: International Universities Press.

WALLERSTEIN, R. (1966): "The Current State of Psychotherapy," *Journal of the American Psychoanalytic Association,* 14:183-225.

————. (1969): "Introduction to Panel on Psychoanalysis and Psychotherapy," *International Journal of Psycho-Analysis,* 50:117-126.

WHITAKER, C., AND T. MALONE. (1953): *The Roots of Psychotherapy.* Philadelphia: Blakiston.

WHITEHEAD, A. N. (1941): *Process and Reality.* New York: Social Science Books.

WIEGERT, E. (1954): "Countertransference and the Self-Analysis of the Psychoanalyst," *International Journal of Psycho-Analysis,* 35:242-246.

WITTGENSTEIN, L. (1953): *Tractatus Logico-Philosophicus.* New York: Humanities Press.

————. (1955): *Philosophical Investigations.* New York: Macmillan.

WOLBERG, L. (1954): *The Technique of Psychotherapy.* New York: Grune and Stratton.

ZELIGS, M. "Acting In," *Journal of the American Psychoanalytic Association,* 5:685-706, 1957.

ZILBOORG, G. (1941): *A History of Medical Psychology.* New York: W. W. Norton and Co.

A Note on the Type

The text of this book was set in Janson, derived from type cast from matrices long thought to have been made by the Dutchman Anton Janson, who was a practicing type founder in Leipzig during the years 1668–87. However, it has been conclusively demonstrated that these types are actually the work of Nicholas Kis (1650–1702), a Hungarian, who most probably learned his trade from the master Dutch type founder Kirk Voskens. The type is an excellent example of the influential and sturdy Dutch types that prevailed in England up to the time William Caslon developed his own incomparable designs from these Dutch faces.

Typography, printing, and binding by The Haddon Craftsmen, Inc., Scranton, Pennsylvania.

FORMAT BY HARVEY DUKE